The European Monetary System: Developments and Perspectives

By Horst Ungerer, Jouko J. Hauvonen,
Augusto Lopez-Claros, and Thomas Mayer

International Monetary Fund
Washington, D.C.
November 1990

Library of Congress Cataloging-in-Publication Data

The European monetary system : developments and perspectives / by
  Horst Ungerer . . . [et al.].
    p. cm. — (Occasional paper ; no. 73)
    Includes bibliographical references.
    ISBN 1-55775-172-2
1. Money—European Economic Community countries. 2. Monetary
policy—European Economic Community countries. I. Ungerer,
Horst. II. Series: Occasional paper (International Monetary Fund) ;
no. 73.
HG930.5E86855 1990   90-21709
332.4'94—dc20   CIP

Price: US$10.00
(US$7.50 university faculty members and students)

Please send orders to:
External Relations Department, Publication Services
International Monetary Fund, Washington, D.C. 20431
Tel: (202) 623-7430   Telefax: (202) 623-7201

Contents

Debate About Future Monetary Integration in the EC
The Delors Report
    Summary of the Delors Report
    The Delors Report and the Werner Report
Discussion of the Delors Report
    The U.K. Proposals for EMU
    Coordination of Fiscal Policies
    Central Bank Independence
Implementation of Stage One and Intergovernmental Conference on EMU

CHARTS

Section

III.

The following symbols have been used throughout this paper:

...   to indicate that data are not available;

—   to indicate that the figure is zero or less than half the final digit shown, or that the item does not exist;

–   between years or months (e.g., 1984–85 or January–June) to indicate the years or months covered, including the beginning and ending years or months;

/   between years (e.g., 1985/86) to indicate a crop or fiscal (financial) year.

"Billion" means a thousand million.

Minor discrepancies between constituent figures and totals are due to rounding.

Preface

On March 13, 1991 it will be twelve years since the European Monetary System (EMS) came into operation. Two earlier studies on EMS developments up to 1986 discussed the background and basic features of the system, reviewed its institutional evolution and exchange market developments, and provided an empirical analysis of exchange rate variability and the convergence of key economic variables (see Ungerer, Evans, and Nyberg (1983) and Ungerer and others (1986)). This study updates and complements those papers. In addition, it surveys financial integration in the European Community (EC) and the present debate about monetary integration, with particular attention to the proposals of the Delors Committee on Economic and Monetary Union.

Events and developments are generally covered through July 1990, but recent events of special interest have been taken into account. Statistical information as a rule includes the year 1989. Literature about the EMS and monetary integration has grown rapidly over the last several years. In this study, reference can only be made to selected samples (for literature up to 1986, see the bibliography of Deville (1986)).

No attempt has been made in this study to assess developments in Central and Eastern Europe since 1989 (including German unification) and their possible implications for the process of financial and monetary integration in the EC. Although over time the political and economic consequences of these events may be quite significant, analysis of them would go beyond the scope of this study. Similarly, the efforts to create a European Economic Space (EES), which would bring the economies of the EC and the European Free Trade Area (EFTA) countries closer together, are not discussed here. Interested readers may want to refer to Occasional Paper No. 74, *The Impact of the European Community's Internal Market on the EFTA*.

This study was prepared by the European Department. Its authors are grateful for helpful comments from colleagues inside and outside the department; special thanks are due to Garry J. Schinasi, who provided the chronology in Appendix III. The authors gratefully acknowledge editorial assistance by Elin Knotter of the External Relations Department, research assistance by Behrouz Guerami and Maha Amad, and secretarial support, in particular by Mary Riegel. They bear sole responsibility for any remaining errors. The views expressed do not necessarily reflect those of the IMF.

I Introduction

When the European Monetary System (EMS) started operating on March 13, 1979, it was seen by some as an engine to foster economic integration in the European Community (EC) and as an important step toward the political unification of Europe and by others as a misguided attempt to force unity on a group of countries where diversity predominated. While the first group saw monetary and economic union close at hand, the second feared that national economic policies might either lose room for maneuver or that the EMS might collapse at an early stage. In the event, the EMS proved to be quite resilient and contributed to progress toward the twin objectives of "greater [monetary] stability at home and abroad,"[1] that is, a high degree of exchange rate stability under conditions of economic convergence at low levels of inflation, thus providing the basis for further progress in financial and monetary integration.

It has been frequently emphasized that without certain beneficial external developments (in particular the appreciation of the U.S. dollar in the system's early years), the EMS would have faced periods of great and possibly destabilizing tension. Also, that there has been a general trend among major countries toward price stability, not limited to the EMS area. Others have argued, however, that without the systemic constraints of the EMS and common economic and political interests, the EMS countries would not have been able to bridge existing differences in economic philosophy, and to cope successfully with such exogenous shocks as the second round of energy price increases in the late 1970s.

While inflation differentials between major industrial countries indeed narrowed during the 1980s, exchange rates between the currencies of those countries experienced strong fluctuations. These fluctuations may not always have been justified by changes in economic fundamentals and therefore resulted in distortions of demand and of the structure of industry of the economies concerned. In contrast, exchange rates within the exchange rate mechanism (ERM)[2] of the EMS followed in broad terms the development of fundamentals. Several realignments compensated largely for cost and price differentials, avoided overshooting and misalignments, and over the longer term permitted real exchange rates to maintain a high degree of stability. In recent years, the countries participating in the ERM succeeded in achieving a high degree of convergence in price and cost developments, allowing their central rates to remain unchanged for extended periods. Stability in nominal and real rates is, of course, one of the key objectives of the EMS and an important element in the renewed efforts of the EC to proceed with economic integration and to create a truly common market, as envisaged in the Single European Act of 1987.

The EMS has at times been described as a regional Bretton Woods system or, alternatively, as not much more than an enlarged "snake," as the European common margins arrangement of the 1970s was called. Neither characterization is correct. In contrast to the Bretton Woods system, the EMS did not start out with a clearly defined center such as gold or the U.S. dollar. Also, it has a common decision-making process for determining exchange rate parities; the original IMF Articles of Agreement provided only for rejection of, or "concurrence" with, a unilaterally proposed parity change. Furthermore, the EMS is based not only on a common interest in a stable exchange rate system but its member countries also share the more far-reaching objectives of economic integration and political cooperation.

The merits of the snake have sometimes been underrated. It is true that in its later years it had shrunk to a number of smaller currencies grouped around the

---

[1] Resolution of the European Council of December 5, 1978 on the establishment of the European Monetary System and related matters in Commission of the European Communities (1979), pp. 95–97.

[2] Belgium-Luxembourg, Denmark, France, Germany, Ireland, Italy, the Netherlands, Spain (since June 1989), and the United Kingdom (since October 1990) participate in the ERM. Throughout this paper the term ERM refers to the mechanism, the participating countries therein, or their currencies. The term EMS is used in more general contexts. All EC countries are members of the EMS. All references to Germany are to the Federal Republic of Germany as it existed before October 3, 1990 when unification took place.

1

deutsche mark. Yet, for this group, it provided a degree of monetary coherence and exchange rate stability that, in the wake of the oil shock of 1973, was strongly lacking in the EC as a whole. It also provided an opportunity for extensive "dress rehearsals" for central bank cooperation in managing a complicated multilateral exchange rate system. This was an important basis for the smooth operational functioning of the EMS as a historically unprecedented exercise in effective cooperation between central banks of different size, varying degrees of autonomy, and differing traditions in terms of operation and policy orientation. What the snake lacked in particular in its early years was a generally accepted economic policy strategy under which exchange rate changes would have been accompanied by domestic adjustment measures, a strategy which in the EMS has allowed simultaneous progress toward external and internal stability. Whereas the snake—not in its original intentions, as envisaged in the Werner Plan, but in its actual realization after the breakdown of the Bretton Woods system in 1973—was limited to being an exchange rate arrangement, the EMS aimed at exchange rate stability through the convergence of economic performance. From the outset, the EMS has not been limited to monetary policy but has aimed at broader objectives of economic integration. It is perhaps this aspect that has helped the EMS through a number of difficult periods. One could argue that without the EMS and its achievements, there would not be a Single European Act in its present form, nor could the EC have moved so decisively toward the complete liberalization of capital movements and the full integration of financial services.

One can distinguish three phases in the development of the EMS.[3] The first, from its beginning in March 1979 to March 1983, can be seen as a phase of trial and orientation. A common economic policy strategy was not yet in place, and the member countries tried to cope with exogenous disturbances in different ways (see Tables 1 and 2 in Appendix I). As a result, divergences in economic developments did not diminish but actually increased in a number of respects. Several realignments—seven including the one in March 1983 (Tables 3–5)—took place to compensate, at least in part, for price and cost differentials. The earlier realignments were generally agreed without much critical introspection and were not accompanied by comprehensive domestic stabilization measures. During this phase, the EMS indeed resembled the snake.

During those early years the ECU (European cur-

rency unit) failed to gain the importance that had been widely hoped for. It did not play a major role either as a reserve asset or as a means of settlement of intervention debts; its function was increasingly limited to that of a unit of account. The European Council Resolution of December 1978 envisaged the consolidation of the EMS after two years into a final stage, which was to entail the creation of a European Monetary Fund and the full utilization of the ECU as a reserve asset and means of settlement. That stage was postponed indefinitely, however.

The second phase, from March 1983 to 1987, can be described as one of consolidation. Economic policies in ERM countries were increasingly oriented toward internal monetary stability. Realignments—or, more precisely, the size of realignments—were regarded not only as an instrument to compensate for past divergences of costs and prices but also—in combination with domestic adjustment measures—as a tool to achieve greater financial discipline and to minimize future divergences. An important milestone in this process was the comprehensive realignment of March 21, 1983 in which the central rates for all ERM currencies were changed (see Table 3). On this occasion, the French Government decided to abandon an unsustainable, expansionary economic policy, to accept in agreement with its partner countries a significant downward shift in the central rate of the French franc against most other ERM currencies (the largest, 8 percent, against the deutsche mark), and to implement a comprehensive package of stabilization measures. The stabilization program, supported by a credit under the community loan mechanism of the EC, was successfully implemented.

The emergence of a common economic policy approach had its corollary in the operational field. The deutsche mark, as the currency with the most consistent record of stability among the major ERM currencies and in its role as reserve currency, emerged as the "anchor currency" of the EMS. German monetary policy, geared toward price stability, assumed a central role as the monetary authorities of the other ERM countries increasingly sought to establish a close exchange rate link to the deutsche mark. This policy allowed them in effect to import stability and to provide their own stabilization efforts with a high degree of credibility. The instrument to achieve this was (voluntary) intramarginal intervention in deutsche mark that increasingly took the place of (obligatory) intervention at the fluctuation margins, which, under the EMS Agreement, had been envisaged as the main method of intervention.

Until September 1987, intramarginal intervention did not qualify for automatic access to the very short-term financing facility (VSTF) of the EMS (the network of

---

[3] For a detailed discussion of the first decade of EMS experience, see Ungerer (1990a). See also Commission of the European Communities (1989a) and Deutsche Bundesbank (1989).

mutual, unlimited credit lines between the participating central banks), prompting countries that relied heavily on intramarginal intervention to seek an extension of the financing arrangements to cover it also. The so-called Basle/Nyborg agreement of September 1987, reached after long discussion among the EMS central banks, provided this possibility within certain limits. It also called for a more flexible use of the fluctuation margins and concerted interest rate adjustments.[4]

The Basle/Nyborg agreement marked the end of the consolidation phase, characterized by the striving for stability, the emergence of the deutsche mark as the anchor currency, and the predominance of intramarginal intervention in partner currencies. At the same time, the agreement also opened a new phase—which involved re-examining various aspects of the management of the system. Some countries argued that the system was working asymmetrically, by granting advantages to the German economy and by placing a disproportionate burden in the adjustment process on the economies with weaker currencies. Italy and France, in particular, called for changes in the way the system was being managed and policy priorities in the EMS were being determined.[5] Furthermore, the question was raised whether the cooperative framework of the EMS should be replaced by commonly defined policies in the monetary and exchange rate fields. In the wake of the adoption of the Single European Act in 1987, with its focus on the completion of the internal market, and the decision by the EC in June 1988 to liberalize fully capital movements, generally by July 1990, the discussion on how to modify the EMS has transformed itself more and more into a debate on whether the EMS as a system will be strong enough to meet the challenges of the internal market.

The answers to these questions were, not surprisingly, far from unanimous. They ranged from the view that the EMS in its present form was well placed to meet future challenges if it was "hardened" (that is, if the common striving for convergence toward internal stability was sufficiently intensified) to the opinion that the successful functioning of the internal market required a more radical approach. According to the latter view, a system of coordination, such as the EMS, would not suffice in an integrated financial market. The EMS should therefore be replaced by common policies and institutions and—eventually but in the not too distant future—by a common single currency.

The debate on how best to organize monetary cooperation and integration in the EC continues. The EC countries have agreed on an intergovernmental conference, to start on December 14, 1990, in Rome, which will deal with questions of economic and monetary union (EMU) and where many of the open issues will have to be addressed.

---

[4] For further details, see Section II.

[5] For further discussion of asymmetry, see Section II.

II Development of the EMS

This section reviews the evolution of the EMS, in particular its membership and how the exchange rate and intervention mechanism has been managed, and describes the institutional changes that have taken place. It also surveys briefly the debate about the system's "asymmetry" and some of the proposals that have been offered as a remedy.

Membership

While from the beginning Belgium-Luxembourg, Denmark, France, Germany, Ireland, Italy, and the Netherlands have participated in all aspects of the EMS, including the ERM, the United Kingdom did not find it advisable to participate fully. It signed the EMS Agreement and, as did other EMS members, deposited 20 percent of its holdings in gold and U.S. dollars in exchange for an equivalent amount of ECUs with the European Monetary Cooperation Fund (EMCF).[6] Also, from the start, sterling was part of the basket of currencies that defined the ECU. But the United Kingdom did not become a participant in the ERM—the heart of the EMS—and was therefore not committed to observing obligatory intervention points for its currency vis-à-vis other EMS currencies. Consequently, it was not a party to the network of mutual credit lines, the VSTF. Together with all other EC members, it takes part in the other credit facilities of the EC—the short-term monetary support, the medium-term financial assistance, and the community loan mechanism (the latter two were merged in the medium-term financial support in 1988; see below). The main reason for not participating in the ERM, according to the U.K. authorities, was their desire to safeguard independence in the pursuit of monetary policy and to retain room for maneuver in view of the pound's role as a "petrocurrency" and as an internationally traded currency. More recently, the relatively high rate of inflation and high interest rates in the United Kingdom were also cited as additional reasons.[7] In the meantime, the U.K. authorities decided to have the pound sterling participate in the ERM effective October 8, 1990, opting temporarily for the wider fluctuation margins of ± 6 percent around bilateral central rates (instead of ± 2.25 percent).

The three countries that joined the EC in the 1980s—Greece in 1981, and Spain and Portugal in 1986—signed the EMS Agreement and thus became in general terms members of the EMS, although they did not immediately join the ERM. The chief reasons for not joining initially were the high inflation rates prevailing in those three countries and, particularly for Greece and Portugal, the pronounced structural differences in their economies from those of the other EC countries. It was feared that participation in the ERM could make frequent changes of their central rates necessary, or impede policies aimed at structural improvements and at lowering the high unemployment rates. Spain, however, at various times indicated a strong interest in participating fully in the EMS as soon as circumstances allowed, and it decided to participate in the ERM as of June 19, 1989. In doing so, it availed itself of the option of temporarily using wider fluctuation margins of ± 6 percent around bilateral central rates.

In the debate surrounding the decision to liberalize capital movements and the question of how the EMS could be strengthened, other EC countries—in particular Germany and France—had frequently called on the United Kingdom to join the ERM while showing understanding for the particular difficulties of the other countries remaining outside the ERM. The report of the Delors Committee (see Section V below) explicitly called for all EC currencies to be included in the ERM during the proposed first stage of efforts toward economic and monetary union.

In the same context, Italy was reminded that maintaining larger fluctuation margins around bilateral central rates was meant to be transitional. Therefore, it was said, Italy should as soon as possible accept the

---

[6] The EMCF was established in April 1973. It has served mainly as the administrator for various transactions under the European common margins arrangement and the EMS, in particular the VSTF.

[7] See Bank of England (1989) and Leigh-Pemberton (1989).

same margins of ± 2.25 percent as other ERM participants. As of January 8, 1990, Italy decided to combine a devaluation of the lira's central rate by 3.7 percent against the ERM partner currencies with the adoption of the narrower margins.

Furthermore, the dual exchange market as practiced by Belgium and Luxembourg (which carried the possibility of different market rates for current and capital transactions) was seen as incompatible with the exchange rate objectives of the EMS. In the context of the liberalization of capital movements, the two countries undertook to abolish the dual market by the end of 1992, and on March 2, 1990 the Belgian-Luxembourg Exchange Institute announced the abolition of the dual exchange market with effect from March 5, 1990.

Recently, Austria and Norway have indicated an interest in a formal association with the EMS,[8] although for the time being no decision has been taken in this respect. In this context, it should be recalled that until December 1978 Norway was associated with the snake, and that for a number of years, Austria has shadowed EMS developments by tying its currency to the deutsche mark. On October 19, 1990, the Norwegian Government decided to peg the Norwegian krone to the ECU effective October 22. The central rate was set at ECU 1 = NKr 7.9940, with a fluctuation margin of ± 2.25 percent of the central rate. It was announced, however, that the Norwegian central bank may refrain from intervening when the deviation exceeds the fluctuation margin.

Evolution

Exchange Rate and Intervention Mechanism

The EMS Agreement of March 1979 envisaged obligatory intervention in partner currencies at the fluctuation margins as the main instrument to ensure the stability of agreed exchange rates. Such obligatory intervention qualified for unlimited financing by the respective partner central banks through the EMCF in the framework of the VSTF. Intervention in partner currencies within the margins was subject to agreement by the central bank issuing the currency to be used and had to be financed out of reserve holdings of that currency or by special bilateral credits outside the VSTF. For purposes of intramarginal intervention,

central banks did not have automatic access to the VSTF; financing through that facility was only possible with the concurrence of the central banks directly involved.

Within a relatively short time, intramarginal intervention became the rule rather than the exception. Most ERM central banks preferred to keep the exchange rate of their currency well within the margins, to forestall in case of temporary weakness any speculative attacks. For this purpose, in the early years of the EMS, they mainly used dollars for intervention, which represented a large part of their international reserves and could be used without the consent of partner central banks. An additional difficulty was that, according to the EMS Agreement, holdings in partner currencies were to be limited to "working balances." Intervention at the margins continued to be undertaken chiefly if a country wanted to gain access to the VSTF and (with sometimes large amounts) at times of strong market pressure that often foreshadowed a realignment of central rates.[9]

In recent years, a broad consensus on economic and monetary policy priorities has developed among the ERM countries. Exchange rate stability and price stability have become twin objectives. Realignments have been used to offset cost and price differentials but have been supported by internal adjustment measures signaling the determination of the authorities to make price stability the priority of economic policy. To stress this point, some countries did not seek full compensation for accrued price and cost differentials in realignments but used an appreciation of their real exchange rate to exert disciplinary pressure on their economies, in particular with regard to budgetary and wage policies ("hard currency policy").[10] To what degree certain currencies did indeed appreciate in real terms as a result of such policies has been subject to some debate, depending on the indicators used in such analyses. Another issue under discussion has been whether and to what degree such changes in the real rate, if they took place, have caused or contributed to existing current account imbalances within the EC (see Section III below).

---

[8] Section A.5.2. of the European Council Resolution of December 1978 provides for the possibility of participation in the exchange rate and intervention mechanism of the EMS for "European countries with particularly close and financial ties" with the EC.

[9] No complete information on the amounts and methods of intervention by ERM countries is available. Giavazzi (1989) provides a table surveying the intervention behavior of the five larger ERM central banks for January 1983–April 1986. The Deutsche Bundesbank, in its annual reports, publishes information on intervention in deutsche mark, with a breakdown according to obligatory and intramarginal intervention. For a summary, see Table 6.

[10] The considerations for such a policy for Italy were stated by Carlo A. Ciampi, Governor of the Bank of Italy, in a speech on January 26, 1988; see Ciampi (1988), p. 59. For case studies of disinflation policy in Italy and Ireland, see Gressani, Guiso, and Visco (1988) and Kremers (1990). On Ireland, see also Jones (1990).

In the operational field, this consensus on the priority of stability-oriented policies found its counterpart in the increased recourse to intramarginal intervention in partner currencies. Several countries undertook to maintain a stable exchange rate relationship to the deutsche mark, among the major currencies the one with the most consistent record of stability in the EC. Monetary policies in those countries were increasingly geared to securing a close link to the deutsche mark, thus making it in practice the anchor currency of the EMS and the point of orientation for monetary policy.[11] In this way, a number of countries with weaker currencies were able to import stability and to gain credibility in their quest for internal stability. In line with market assessments of the strengths of individual currencies, central banks maintained varying interest rate differentials vis-à-vis German rates.

The German authorities initially were quite reluctant to have their currency assume such a central role in the EMS because they were wary of possible risks to their own monetary policy. In particular, the accumulation of large deutsche mark holdings by other central banks was seen as a potential threat to monetary control in Germany. But over time they increasingly accepted intramarginal interventions in their currency. Since such transactions were financed with funds purchased by the intervening central bank in the market during earlier periods of deutsche mark weakness, they did not add to the existing aggregate supply of deutsche mark, in contrast to interventions at the margins. Consequently, the German authorities came to interpret liberally the limiting rule on the holding of working balances in deutsche mark, to agree more readily to, and at times to encourage, the use of their currency for intramarginal intervention.

The consensus on economic policy priorities, the increasing convergence of key nominal variables, and the mostly successful management of exchange rates, intervention, and interest rate differentials go a long way toward explaining why for more than three years (from March 1983 until April 1986) there was no general realignment of central rates in the EMS (Table 3). In addition, the strength of the dollar during this period helped to minimize tensions in the system. The bilateral devaluations of the Italian lira in July 1985 and of the Irish pound in August 1986 were related to special developments.[12]

Another general, relatively small, realignment took place on January 12, 1987, involving the revaluation of the deutsche mark, the Netherlands guilder, and the Belgian and Luxembourg francs against the other ERM currencies. There was broad agreement at the time that the realignment was neither caused nor justified by divergences in economic performance but mainly triggered by international developments, in particular the steady fall of the dollar during 1986 and in the first weeks of 1987, but also by domestic developments in France (see Section III below).

No realignment of central rates took place from January 1987 to January 1990, when the Italian lira was devalued by a moderate amount against other ERM currencies (see Section III). This marked the longest period without any changes in the parity grid of the ERM. The general, though not uncontested, view was that developments in international competitiveness in ERM countries did not justify any exchange rate action, and that any emerging pressure on exchange rates could satisfactorily be dealt with by the use of other policy instruments. It is also interesting to note that during that period disturbances in international financial markets (the major exception being the Wall Street crash of October 1987) or political events (such as the presidential and parliamentary election in France in May 1988) created little tension within the EMS, in contrast to earlier experience. Similarly, the abolition of remaining capital controls by France and Italy in January and May 1990, respectively, did not lead to any pressure on ERM exchange rates. These developments may in part be attributed to a better management of the system but probably more significantly to a higher degree of credibility of the ERM countries in their pursuit of stability-oriented policies. They also indicate a general acceptance by the market of the determination of the authorities to defend prevailing central rates. Another factor may be the gradual opening and liberalization of financial markets in a number of EC countries, which allowed portfolio diversification by international investors, thus mitigating the impact of a weakening dollar on the relative position of the deutsche mark within the ERM. Furthermore, the financing of existing external imbalances through the markets did not pose any particular problems.

The ECU

The Resolution of the European Council of December 1978,[13] establishing the main features of the EMS, aimed at placing the ECU at the center of the system. In the event, its functions remained quite limited, largely confined to being a unit of account in the context of the EMS and the various financial activities of the EC.

---

[11] Russo and Tullio (1988) refer to "an implicit agreement on inflation . . .—namely, to converge toward the German inflation rate and to let the Federal Republic of Germany determine the anchor inflation rate of the system" (p. 63). On this issue, see also Rieke (1989).

[12] For details, see Section III.

[13] See fn. 1 above.

Several reasons exist for this development. First, the commitment of the EC countries to the ECU was from the beginning less than complete. In its role as a reserve asset and a means of settlement, the ECU was severely limited by a number of factors:

- the creation of ECUs by the EMCF against the deposit of international reserves of EMS central banks was temporary and limited to renewable three-month swaps; the agreement on the creation of ECUs was subject to reconfirmation every two years; and the swapped reserves continued to be administered by the respective central banks;[14]

- in the absence of a market, official ECUs could not be directly used for intervention; their use was confined to the settlement of debts arising from obligatory intervention within the ERM, with an acceptance limit on the use of ECUs of 50 percent, and to bilateral, mutually agreed transactions;

- the evolution of the EMS with its emphasis on intramarginal intervention (first in dollars, then increasingly in currencies participating in the ERM, in particular deutsche mark), greatly diminished the role of the ECU as a means of settlement;

- official ECUs could not be used outside the ERM context;

- the ECU did not become the starting point for the determination of central rates in the ERM: they are determined bilaterally; nor did the divergence indicator, in which the ECU was assigned a central role, acquire any operational significance—partly because of flaws in its construction, partly because of policy.[15]

These factors made the ECU an instrument of limited usefulness and attractiveness. The agreement between EMS central banks of June 1985 sought to enhance the role of the official ECU.[16] It introduced the possibility of participating central banks mobilizing ECUs, within certain limits, to obtain currency for intramarginal intervention. In addition, it made the return on ECU holdings more attractive and provided for the designation of "other holders," which allows monetary institutions outside the EMS to hold official ECUs. But the agreement did little to strengthen the role of the ECU. The mobilization mechanism was used only twice, by the same country. The option to become an other holder was taken up only by the Bank for International Settlements (BIS), the Swiss National Bank, and the Austrian National Bank; this is not surprising considering that official ECUs can be used only in the ERM context. Similarly, the revision of the formula determining the interest rate on ECU holdings did not noticeably enhance the ECU's attractiveness in view

of its limited usability and the way the ERM has been managed.

Another effort to strengthen the role of the ECU was made in the context of the Basle/Nyborg agreement of September 1987 (see below). The possibility of using the VSTF also for financing intramarginal intervention, within prescribed limits, has made the use of ECUs for the settlement of intervention debts more likely.

The currency composition of the ECU was revised as of September 21, 1989 to include the Spanish peseta and the Portuguese escudo. Besides including those two currencies, the new percentage weights also incorporated some reapportionment of the weights of the other ten currencies (Tables 7 and 8). In particular, the inclusion of the peseta and the escudo—with a combined weight of 6.1 percent—was not accompanied by a uniform proportional reduction in the weights of the other currencies, compared with their levels on September 17, 1984.

In contrast to the official ECU, the use of the private ECU, which is a financial instrument defined by the same basket of currencies as the official ECU, experienced rapid growth in its early years. It has been used to hedge against exchange rate risks and to benefit from higher returns on investments in weaker currencies. By now, its use has been permitted in all EC countries, and it is officially recognized as a currency by several EC members. Although capital restrictions in some EC countries applied in principle also to the private ECU, it enjoyed preferential treatment in several EC countries as well as encouragement for its use by some governments and by the EC Commission. More recently, however, the growth of the market in private ECUs—mostly limited to banking transactions—has slowed significantly because the ECU's role as a hedge against exchange rate risks has become less important as the parity grid of the ERM remained unchanged for longer periods, and as the commitment of the authorities to a stable exchange rate pattern gained credibility.[17]

An interesting aspect of the private ECU is that in the last few years some ERM central banks have acquired private ECUs in the market to diversify their portfolios of international reserves and to use them for exchange market intervention in support of their currencies. These practices have raised a number of questions. First, since an ECU also contains a certain amount of the currency for whose support it is used, the net effect of such intervention is more limited than if a national currency is used, especially for currencies with a larger share in the ECU basket. Second, if another partner currency shows concurrent weakness in the market, its

---

[14] For the amounts of ECUs created, see Table 9.
[15] See Ungerer, Evans, and Nyberg (1983), p. 15.
[16] For details, see Ungerer and others (1986), p. 8.

[17] For a more detailed discussion of the private ECU, see International Monetary Fund (1987), Istituto Bancario San Paolo di Torino, *ECU Newsletter*, various issues, and Levich (1987).

exchange rate will become even more depressed by the sale of the private ECUs by the first country. These considerations point to rather narrow limits for the use of private ECUs for intervention, depending on the width of the foreign exchange market at a given time, the position of other currencies in the ERM band, and the weight of currencies in the ECU basket. So far, however, the use of private ECUs by central banks has been fairly limited, and no risk for the proper functioning of the ERM has been seen.[18]

Credit Facilities[19]

The short-term monetary support and the medium-term financial assistance (MTFA) have not been used since the beginning of the EMS. There have been two loans under the community loan mechanism (CLM). The limited role of the credit facilities could be explained by the use of exchange rate policy in helping to correct unsustainable imbalances in current accounts while the financing of actual current account deficits did not encounter particular problems. Private capital flows of a short-term and long-term nature, encouraged by appropriate interest rate differentials, compensated largely for such deficits. Furthermore, deficit countries did not find it difficult to obtain credits in the international financial markets. This ease of financing may have been enhanced by a market perception of the existence of an EC "umbrella" in the form of the existing credit facilities and the anticipation of some peer pressure within the EC toward domestic adjustment, aimed at reducing economic divergences and thus the further accumulation of current account deficits.

The EC granted financial assistance under the CLM to France in May 1983, in the amount of ECU 4 billion, and to Greece in December 1985, in the amount of ECU 1,750 million.[20] The credit to France was disbursed in one sum and was repaid in advance of maturity. The credit to Greece consisted of two installments; the first was disbursed immediately, and the second was released in December 1986, following a review of the economic recovery program by the Monetary Committee and the Council of Ministers.

In connection with the adoption of the directive on the liberalization of capital movements in the EC in June 1988 (see Section IV), the EC Council of Ministers decided to merge the two conditional medium-term financing facilities, the MTFA and the CLM (established in 1971 and 1975, respectively) in a new facility, the medium-term financial support (MTFS).[21] Since 1985, the creditor commitment ceilings under MTFA have totaled ECU 15.9 billion and the borrowing limit under CLM has been ECU 8 billion. With a view to providing particularly a quickly deployable, flexible, and adequate financial "safety net" in the context of capital liberalization, it has been agreed to meet under the new MTFS possible requests from member countries for balance of payments assistance primarily by means of Community borrowing in financial markets (of up to ECU 14 billion). If market borrowing should prove difficult or has reached the ceiling of ECU 14 billion, the member countries would be requested to contribute the funds needed, subject to country-specific ceilings totaling ECU 13,925 million. The total outstanding amount of lending from the MTFS is subject to a limit of ECU 16 billion. Lending from the facility remains (as under the former MTFA and CLM) subject to conditionality, aimed at re-establishing or ensuring a sustainable balance of payments situation.

Changes in the Institutional Setup

The evolution of the EMS into a system centered on the deutsche mark as anchor currency raised concerns in some countries. There was not only the desire to give the EMS a stronger institutional framework but also the concern that the actual management of the system impeded growth, that the burden of intervention (for example, obtaining the required currencies and the necessary agreement for their use) was placed on weaker currencies, and that the policy vis-à-vis the dollar was in fact set by the Bundesbank.

The events of late 1986 and early 1987, when the authorities of ERM countries were forced, chiefly by international exchange market developments rather than by the development of intra-ERM fundamentals, to carry out a realignment, helped to crystalize such feelings. At the conclusion of the realignment meeting on January 12, 1987, the EC ministers of economics and finance requested the Committee of Central Bank Governors and the Monetary Committee to examine measures to strengthen the operating mechanisms of the EMS. Both committees discussed extensively a wide range of proposals. In a meeting in Basle in September 1987, the EC central bank governors agreed on a set of measures, and this agreement was endorsed by

---

[18] For a further discussion of private ECU interventions, see Moss (1988). About the prospects for the private ECU in the context of further integration of financial markets see, inter alia, Folkerts-Landau and Mathieson (1989).

[19] Credit facilities, except the VSTF, are for the use of all EC members. For details, see Ungerer, Evans, and Nyberg (1983), p. 17, and Ungerer and others (1986), p. 6.

[20] For details, see Ungerer and others (1986), p. 6.

[21] *Official Journal of the European Communities* (henceforth OJ), L 178, July 8, 1988.

the economics and finance ministers at their meeting in Nyborg of September 12, 1987.[22]

The Basle/Nyborg agreement consists of the following elements:

(1) intensified surveillance on the basis of indicators and projections by the Monetary Committee and the Committee of Central Bank Governors, in particular to highlight any policy inconsistencies between EMS countries and incompatible approaches vis-à-vis third currencies;

(2) more emphasis on the use of interest rate differentials for the defense of the grid of ERM central rates;

(3) flexible use of the fluctuation margins to deter speculation and to avoid intramarginal intervention over longer periods;

(4) less frequent and smaller realignments;

(5) the possibility of financing intramarginal intervention through recourse to the VSTF, subject to certain quantitative limits and other conditions;

(6) increasing the acceptance limit for ECUs in the settlement of intervention debts from 50 to 100 percent for a trial period of two years;[23]

(7) extending the basic time limit for borrowing under the VSTF by one month to three and a half months, and doubling the ceiling applied to the automatic renewal for three months of such financing operations.

The communiqué of the meeting of the ministers emphasized that the agreement would "officialize" intramarginal intervention, which had not been explicitly envisaged in the original EMS Agreement. It refers to "a new phase for the EMS, creating in a flexible way a better-balanced System while maintaining the primary objective of establishing a greater degree of internal (prices) and external (exchange rates) stability in Europe."

The Basle/Nyborg agreement found a somewhat mixed reception. While in official central bank circles it was considered a balanced package of measures,[24] public opinion in Germany expressed the fear that the obligation to finance intramarginal intervention, even if subject to certain limits, could lead to the excessive creation of liquidity and thus endanger the monetary targets of the Bundesbank. The latter view overlooked, however, that intramarginal intervention remained subject to approval by the central bank issuing the intervention currency; that the amounts involved would be limited in relation to total money supply; and that, unless tension in the ERM was to be resolved by a realignment of central rates, the alternative to intramarginal intervention would be intervention at the margins where the financing obligations would be unlimited in amount. On the other hand, the view in other participating countries was that the agreement did not go far enough and that additional modifications in the operational procedures and the institutional setup of the EMS were needed.

A major test for the usefulness of the Basle/Nyborg agreement came soon after its conclusion, in the wake of the stock market crash on Wall Street in October 1987. The dollar fell rapidly in international exchange markets, and general uncertainty arose about the impact on the U.S. economy and the world economy. A number of countries tried to forestall an anticipated recessionary fallout of the events in stock markets by easing monetary policies. Funds moved out of the United States, which led to tension within the ERM, following past patterns of upward pressure on the deutsche mark relative to other currencies, in particular the French franc. The monetary authorities of France and Germany reacted swiftly by undertaking massive intramarginal intervention, financed to the maximum set in the Basle/Nyborg agreement and by an additional bilateral credit from the Bundesbank to the Bank of France. At the same time, the French franc was allowed to depreciate within the band against the deutsche mark. This action was combined with coordinated interest rate moves, in particular by the central banks of France and Germany, and it was successful. The market accepted that the existing ERM central rates would be maintained, and soon the speculative movements in expectation of a realignment were reversed. Again, during a similar period of tension in August/September 1988, the ERM central banks successfully used the combination of intervention, differentiated interest rate moves, and exchange rate flexibility within the fluctuation margins to reject speculative attacks and defend the ERM parity grid.

Asymmetry in the EMS

The discussions about the further development of the EMS continued after the Basle/Nyborg agreement, and additional questions concerning modification of the EMS Agreement were raised. It was argued by some countries—in particular France and Italy—that the EMS, in its design, its policies, and its operations, was characterized by asymmetry, placing a larger burden for its management on the countries with weaker currencies.[25] In the operational field, the technique of

---

[22] See texts of communiqués in Appendix II.
[23] In the meantime, it has been made permanent.
[24] See, for example, Szász (1988).

[25] See the memoranda by the finance ministers of France and Italy at that time, Balladur (1988) and Amato (1988). For a response, see Gleske (1988).

For a discussion in academic circles, see, for example, Wyplosz (1988a and 1988b), Russo and Tullio (1988), De Grauwe (1989), and Portes (1989).

intramarginal intervention, which helped the system to maintain stability, was said to lead to asymmetry, since it was up to all ERM central banks except the one issuing the anchor currency to undertake the required intervention. Even in the case of intervention at the margins, where both sides have to intervene, there was asymmetry insofar as debtor central banks would be the ones to lose reserves. With regard to monetary policy and interventions vis-à-vis third currencies, it was the leading central bank, the Bundesbank, that determined the course of action, and all other central banks had to follow if balance within the ERM was to be maintained. It was the dominant country in the EMS—Germany—that determined the general orientation of economic policy in the EMS. This narrowed the choice of economic strategies for its partner countries, impeded growth-oriented policies on their part, and thus perpetuated unemployment problems. Last, the hegemonic role of German economic policy was contrary to the community character of the EMS.

To remedy the perceived imperfections in the way the EMS operated, several proposals were made. Intramarginal intervention should be eligible for automatic financing in the framework of the VSTF without limitations. Intramarginal intervention should be undertaken by stronger as well as weaker currencies, and there should be mutual holdings of partner currencies among the ERM central banks. The general direction of monetary policies should be commonly decided, and a common dollar policy should be implemented. The idea arose of doing away with the anchor role of the deutsche mark by basing the intervention mechanism—as contemplated during the planning phase of the EMS—on the ECU, and of using a mechanism to identify divergences and to determine adjustment measures symmetrically—a reinforced divergence indicator, as it were.

Some member countries were satisfied with the way the EMS worked and emphasized that the best way to strengthen it was to continue with stability-oriented policies and to strive for a higher degree of convergence in economic performance. Intramarginal intervention was the choice of the countries undertaking it and was not inherent to the system, while obligatory intervention with its consequential creation of additional liquidity by the strong-currency countries often carried for them the danger of upsetting their domestic monetary objectives. The mutual holding of reserves would amount to additional financing, in particular as long as the weaker currencies were not accepted by the market as reserve currencies. A "softening" of monetary policies would only weaken the coherence of the EMS. The EMS needed an anchor, and it should be the currency with the best record of stability. The leading role of German monetary policy was just the mirror image

of the credibility that the German anchor lent to the anti-inflationary policies of Germany's partner countries. Indeed, the only way to replace the anchor currency would be to introduce a common policy, but this step would be unacceptable as long as economic policies and developments did not sufficiently and irreversibly converge toward price stability.

From an economic point of view, the various arguments surrounding the problem of asymmetry—whether in the operational or in the policy field—could essentially be reduced to two issues. One is fairly familiar and was intensively discussed in connection with the creation of the SDR scheme and during the final period of the Bretton Woods system: it is the question of the relative weight of financing and of adjustment in addressing imbalances. The other concerns the priorities of economic policy, in particular the relative importance of price stability compared with greater emphasis on growth and higher employment—if such a trade-off exists. The latter issue also raises the question of the effectiveness of demand management policies with regard to unemployment in view of existing structural problems and rigidities.

It is interesting that the debate about asymmetry has been conducted largely under the implicit assumption of no changes in ERM central rates. In this way, the possibility of decoupling one economy from the other by way of exchange rate adjustments was not explicitly discussed. This seemed to reflect a difference in importance attached to the objectives of "external" (exchange rate) stability, versus "internal" (price) stability. It also reflected the dilemma of a weaker-currency country that questions the economic policy of the leading country. While a change in parity vis-à-vis the leading country could enlarge the scope for independent policy action, it could also erode the economic policy credibility of the weak-currency country that has been achieved over time by tying its exchange rate and monetary policy to this very country. Conversely, the strong-currency country might not have been in favor of a shift in exchange rates, because it would weaken export-led growth and intensify structural difficulties in certain industries and regions.

The debate about asymmetry muted somewhat in 1989 and 1990. Inflation has again been on the rise, and it has become apparent that the degree of capacity utilization and sectoral bottlenecks in the labor markets in most ERM countries did not allow economic policies to be reoriented in an expansionary direction. As to future developments, a consensus has emerged that for the core participants in the ERM—in this context seen to include Belgium, France, Germany, Luxembourg, and the Netherlands—a change in central rates has become unlikely. In general, the discussion about the working of the EMS has acquired an altogether new dimension: whether the EMS was sufficiently equipped to meet the future challenges of a single internal market in the EC, in particular of integrated financial markets with full liberalization of capital movements, and how best to move toward economic and monetary union in the EC. Nevertheless, the basic issues of asymmetry—financing versus adjustment in case of imbalances, and the priorities of economic policy—have remained very much on the agenda, no matter how monetary cooperation in the EC may be organized.

III Economic Performance

Exchange Rate Developments: Trends and Issues

During the early years of the EMS there were frequent periods of tension within the ERM that gave rise to a number of realignments (Table 3). These developments reflected the persistence of significant differences among member countries as regards economic policy objectives and performance and the tendency to rely on exchange rate adjustments to correct underlying macroeconomic imbalances (Table 2). At the same time, asymmetric capital flows in periods of dollar weakness, with funds flowing primarily into the deutsche mark, contributed to tension within the system. Since March 1983, however, there have been extended periods characterized by exchange rate stability and the absence of realignments. This period witnessed an increasing degree of convergence in the stance of monetary policies of member countries and a sustained narrowing of price and cost differentials, reflecting an emerging consensus on the priorities of economic policy and, in particular, the need for price stability. It also witnessed an increased readiness to use policy instruments other than the exchange rate to address macroeconomic imbalances. Through either greater fiscal restraint, the increasingly unaccommodating stance of monetary policies, or wage moderation, the role of domestic policies in the adjustment process was enhanced. This situation in turn introduced an element of discipline to economic policy formulation. At the operational level it found expression in the increasing reliance on intramarginal intervention as a means of stabilizing exchange rates relative to the deutsche mark, the anchor currency of the EMS. The combination of increased emphasis within the ERM countries on policies aimed at establishing a noninflationary macroenvironment and of intervention policies aimed at stabilizing market exchange rates over time contributed to enhancing the credibility of the system (Chart 1).

The Realignments of 1985–86

The period from 1983 to 1986 nevertheless did witness three realignments: the July 1985 devaluation of

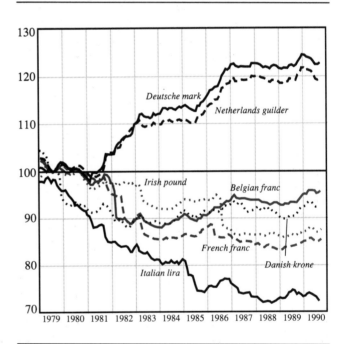

Chart 1. ERM: Movements of Exchange Rates Against the ECU

(Monthly averages, July 1979 = 100)

Source: International Monetary Fund, *International Financial Statistics.*

the Italian lira, the general realignment of April 1986, and the August 1986 devaluation of the Irish pound. The Italian lira adjustment followed a period of deterioration in the current account linked to relatively high rates of growth of domestic demand and an erosion of external competitiveness. The lira was devalued by 6 percent on July 22, and the other participating currencies revalued by 2 percent, implying a close to 8 percent downward shift of the lira vis-à-vis the other ERM currencies. The April 6, 1986 general realignment took place on the initiative of the French authorities, who sought a depreciation of the French franc as part of a package of stabilization measures aimed at restoring the economy's external competitiveness. Supporting measures included a slowing of the growth of nominal wages, a reduction in the noninterest component of the budget deficit, and the continued reliance on high interest rates to control the growth of the monetary aggregates. The deutsche mark and the Netherlands guilder were revalued by 3 percent, the Belgian and Luxembourg francs and the Danish krone were revalued by 1 percent, while the French franc was devalued by 3 percent; the Italian lira and the Irish pound remained unchanged. The 8 percent devaluation of the Irish pound that became effective on August 4, 1986 sought to offset a sharp appreciation against sterling and the dollar and the impact this appreciation had had on the evolution of the effective exchange rate of the Irish pound. The United Kingdom and the United States account for nearly 50 percent of Irish trade; capital outflows and a concomitant fall in reserves unsettled financial markets and prompted the Irish authorities to request a change in central rates.[26]

The Plaza Agreement

The further depreciation of the dollar during 1986— 20 percent in nominal effective terms,[27] 22 percent against the ECU (Chart 2)—should be seen against the background of the September 1985 agreement among the countries constituting the Group of Five, when the finance ministers and central bank governors (meeting at the Plaza Hotel in New York) announced the desirability of ''some further orderly appreciation of the main non-dollar currencies against the dollar'' and underscored their willingness to ''cooperate more closely to encourage this when to do so would be helpful.''[28] The depreciation also reflected additional factors, including the continued widening of the current account deficit in the United States, the sharp drop in oil prices, which was relatively more favorable to continental European countries and Japan than to the United States on account of their greater dependence on oil imports, and the more pronounced fall in interest rates in the United States than in most of the larger industrial countries (Charts 3, 4, and 5). Further strong downward pressure in the early part of 1987 appears to have reflected market concern about the absence of improvement in the U.S. current account.

The counterpart of the dollar's fall was an appreciation of the currencies of other industrial countries, including those participating in the ERM. Between the

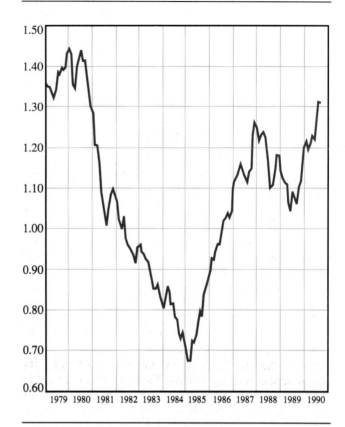

Chart 2. Movements of the ECU Against the U.S. Dollar

(U.S. dollar per ECU, monthly averages)

Source: International Monetary Fund, *International Financial Statistics.*

first quarter of 1986 and the onset of the Louvre Accord (February 1987; see below), the deutsche mark appreciated by 9 percent in nominal effective terms; over the same period the yen appreciated by over 11 percent. In real effective terms the respective appreciations were 8 percent for the deutsche mark and 7 percent for the yen (Chart 6).[29] The upward pressure on the deutsche mark was linked to substantial increases in the German current account surplus (Table 13) and a narrowing of the interest rate differential vis-à-vis the United States (Chart 3).

The January 1987 Realignment

Foreign exchange markets were unsettled in the latter part of 1986 and in early 1987. Notwithstanding

---

[26] For further background information on these three realignments, see Ungerer and others (1986).

[27] Vis-à-vis a group of 17 industrial countries.

[28] As quoted in the official communiqué, reproduced in *IMF Survey,* October 7, 1985, p. 296.

[29] Against a larger set of partner countries that includes a number of producers of primary commodities, the yen's real effective appreciation was more pronounced (11 percent versus 6 percent for the deutsche mark), reflecting Japan's larger share of trade with the United States and with countries with dollar-linked currencies.

Chart 3. Short-Term U.S. Dollar and Deutsche Mark Interest Rates, 1984–90

(In percent per annum)

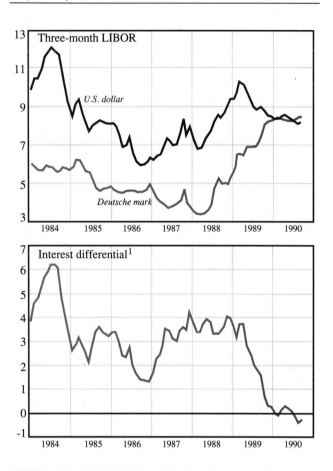

Source: International Monetary Fund, Data Fund.
[1] U.S. dollar rate minus deutsche mark rate.

Chart 4. Short-Term U.S. Dollar and French Franc Interest Rates, 1984–90

(In percent per annum)

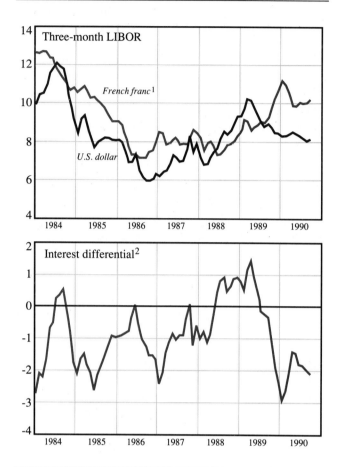

Source: International Monetary Fund, Data Fund.
[1] Interbank money rate.
[2] U.S. dollar rate minus French franc rate.

sizable interventions by the Bundesbank and the Bank of Japan, the dollar continued to fall vis-à-vis the deutsche mark and the yen. As in earlier periods of dollar weakness speculative capital flowed into Germany. At the same time, the French franc came under stress at a time when labor unrest brought pressure to bear on the authorities' policy of wage restraint. The Bank of France reacted initially by intervening in the foreign exchange markets and raising interest rates; when these measures failed to calm speculation about a possible realignment, and pressure on the franc intensified, the Bank of France allowed the franc to fall to its lower intervention limit vis-à-vis the deutsche mark. This triggered obligatory interventions in the ERM to prevent these two currencies from breaching their respective limits. On January 12, 1987 the EC ministers of economics and finance and central bank governors agreed on an adjustment of central rates within the ERM. The deutsche mark and the Dutch guilder were revalued by 3 percent and the Belgian and Luxembourg francs by 2 percent against the French franc and the other ERM currencies. (For movements of currencies within the ERM bands, see Charts 7 and 8.)

Unlike previous exchange rate adjustments in the EMS, the realignment was not brought about by any clear need to offset changes in cost/price competitiveness among participating countries but was rather a response to unequal pressures on some ERM currencies stemming from international capital flows linked to the weakening of the dollar. The absence of capital controls and the presence of relatively well developed financial markets, against a background of price stability, had made the deutsche mark an attractive reserve currency. At the same time, it was felt that the realign-

Chart 5. Short-Term U.S. Dollar and Pound Sterling Interest Rates, 1984–90

(In percent per annum)

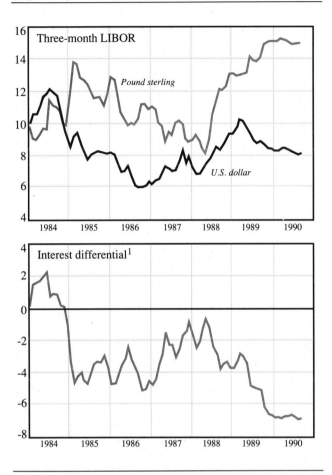

Source: International Monetary Fund, Data Fund.
[1] U.S. dollar rate minus pound sterling rate.

Chart 6. Effective Exchange Rates, 1979–90

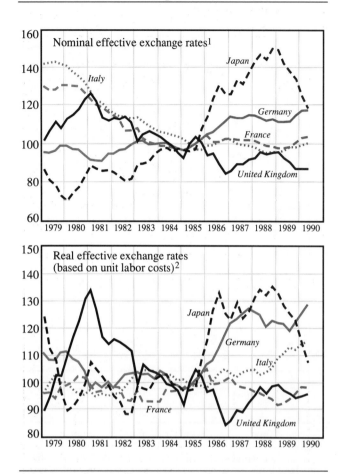

Source: International Monetary Fund, *International Financial Statistics*.
[1] Vis-à-vis 16 industrial countries.
[2] Relative unit labor costs corrected for exchange rate changes.

ment might have been avoided by a better coordination of monetary policies, particularly as regards interest rates. Market perceptions may have also been influenced by continued divergences among ERM countries in external current account performance (Table 13) and the stance of fiscal policy. Such divergences had not adversely affected exchange rate stability in the ERM during the period of increasing dollar strength (particularly 1983–84, through the first quarter of 1985) but became a relatively more important factor as the dollar weakened and other currencies became correspondingly more attractive for investors.

Following the realignment there was a concerted effort within the EC to identify ways to strengthen the operating mechanisms of the EMS, which led to the Basle/Nyborg agreement of September 1987 (see Section II).

The Louvre Accord and Developments in 1987

In the period after the January 1987 realignment, exchange rate developments were influenced by central bank intervention reflecting the agreement reached at the February 1987 meeting in Paris of finance ministers and central bank governors of the six major industrial countries (the so-called Louvre Accord). Concerned that "further substantial exchange rate shifts among their currencies could damage growth and adjustment prospects in their countries," the ministers and governors agreed that exchange rate changes over the previous year and a half had "brought their currencies within ranges broadly consistent with underlying economic fundamentals" and expressed their determination to "cooperate closely to foster stability of exchange rates

Chart 7. EMS: Position in the Narrow Band, 1986–89[1]

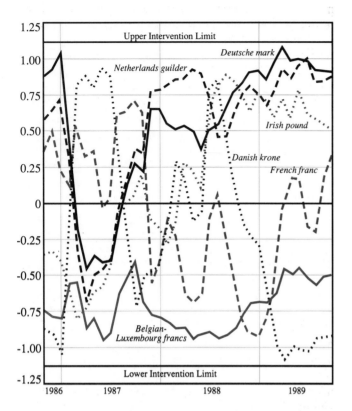

Sources: International Monetary Fund, *International Financial Statistics*, various issues; and Fund staff estimates.
[1] Monthly averages; Italian lira not included. The chart measures deviations of currencies from their bilateral central rates in terms of logarithmic differences between spot exchange rates and bilateral central rates multiplied by 100.

Chart 8. EMS: Position in the Wide Band, 1986–89[1]

Sources: International Monetary Fund, *International Financial Statistics*, various issues; and Fund staff estimates.
[1] Monthly averages. The chart measures deviations of currencies from their bilateral central rates in terms of logarithmic differences between spot exchange rates and bilateral central rates multiplied by 100.

around current levels.''[30] The Louvre Accord was thus seen as a commitment to industrial country cooperation in efforts to stabilize the dollar exchange rate against the yen and the deutsche mark, and hence also vis-à-vis the ERM currencies.[31] The accord came at a time of widening external imbalances. The U.S. current account deficit in 1986 had risen to close to 3½ percent of GDP while the Japanese and German surpluses stood at 4½ percent and 4 percent of GDP, respectively. The official view appears to have been that not only were exchange rate adjustments yet to have a full impact on trade flows but that there was a danger that J-curve

effects[32] might lead to an overshooting in the dollar decline. Furthermore, the process of external adjustment would be facilitated by a number of supporting measures to be implemented by the industrial countries over the period 1987–88. Such measures included fiscal stimulus in Germany and Japan and a reduction in the growth of expenditures and a corresponding narrowing of the fiscal deficit in the United States.

The policy of pursuing exchange rate stability against a background of persistent and sizable external imbalances has not been without its critics. It was argued (Feldstein, 1988), for instance, that the dollar should continue to fall to generate the changes in relative prices needed to induce the required shifts in the patterns of international consumption; in the absence of

[30] As quoted in the official communiqué, reproduced in *IMF Survey*, March 9, 1987, p. 75.
[31] This commitment was reaffirmed by the seven major industrial countries in December 1987, at the Toronto summit in June 1988, and at the IMF/IBRD Annual Meetings in Berlin in September 1988.

[32] A reference to the fact that the immediate effects of an exchange rate change on import and export prices are compensated, only after a lag, by the desired volume effects and thus may lead initially to a deterioration of the current account.

further relative price adjustment the U.S. current account deficit would remain in excess of $100 billion a year in the foreseeable future, owing in part to the increasing burden of interest payments on the U.S. net foreign borrowing. The fiscal stimulus called for in Germany and Japan would not, according to this view, be sufficiently powerful to make a dent in the U.S. current account deficit. Furthermore, an overvalued exchange rate would ultimately slow the process of capital formation and undermine the recovery of manufacturing industries in the United States.[33]

The exchange rate of the dollar against the deutsche mark and other ERM currencies did stabilize in the eight-month period following the Louvre Accord before falling again in the latter part of 1987. This did not happen against the yen, as the dollar continued to fall, with occasional interruptions, to all-time lows by May 1988. Between the first quarter of 1987 and the second quarter of 1988, when the dollar began to rise again, the dollar depreciated by 11 percent in real effective terms. It appears that during much of 1987 private investor reluctance to increase the share of dollar assets in their portfolios led to a sharp increase in official holdings of dollars in amounts roughly equivalent to the size of the U.S. current account deficit.

Renewed tensions appeared within the ERM in the wake of the sharp drop in U.S. stock prices in October 1987. As a weakening of the dollar triggered international capital flows into the deutsche mark, some ERM currencies, particularly the French franc, came under heavy pressure. These challenges were successfully met by cooperative exchange market intervention, well-coordinated interest rate adjustments, particularly between the Deutsche Bundesbank and the Bank of France, and a more extended use of the available fluctuation margins in the ERM (see also Section II above).

Interesting features of the process of currency realignment associated with the decline of the dollar in 1985–88 are the somewhat disparate movements in the effective exchange rates of non-dollar currencies it seems to have entailed (see Chart 6). Taking as benchmarks the first quarter of 1985—when the dollar peaked—and the second quarter of 1988—when it stabilized—the depreciation in real effective terms, using relative unit labor costs, was about 40 percent. The dollar's nominal declines against individual currencies included a 39 percent drop against sterling, 48 percent

---

[33] A further criticism of recent exchange rate management by the major industrial countries is that the discussion has always centered on *nominal* exchange rates. Even if, through intervention and other policy measures, the exchange rate targets were achieved, differences in prices and costs across countries would not prevent shifts in real exchange rates and hence relative competitiveness. It was the evolution of the latter that was relevant for the correction of current account imbalances.

against the deutsche mark, and 51 percent against the yen. But whereas over the same period the deutsche mark had appreciated by 17 percent in real effective terms, the real appreciation of the yen had been close to 34 percent, reflecting the much larger share of Japanese trade with the United States and other countries with currencies linked to the dollar, while German trade is mainly with European trade partners. The real effective exchange rate movements of the other ERM currencies were likewise much less pronounced than those of the dollar and the yen, ranging from virtually no change for France to a 4 percent depreciation for Italy. Among EC currencies, the sharp appreciation of the deutsche mark was only exceeded by sterling, which rose by 19 percent in real terms over the same period.

Developments in 1988–89

Exchange rate developments in 1988–89 took place against a background of continued commitment to exchange rate stability by countries of the Group of Seven. Official intervention in the foreign exchange markets in support of this objective was, in sharp contrast to 1987, in both directions, with no apparent net increase in the official dollar holdings of the main intervening countries.

The strengthening of the dollar that began in mid-1988 reflects a number of factors. The most influential was evidence of a narrowing of the nominal U.S. current account deficit; figures for the trade deficit for the first half of 1988 were particularly encouraging and seemed to suggest that some measure of external adjustment was finally under way. Also of importance was the relatively strong performance of the U.S. economy—with evidence of emerging pressures on resource utilization—and a tightening of the stance of monetary policy against a background of increasing concern about the inflationary impact of further depreciation. A gradual widening of interest rate differentials in favor of dollar-denominated assets induced substantial shifts in the private demand for dollar assets, shifts that were fully reflected in capital account data. Throughout much of 1988 and the first half of 1989 short-term interest rate differentials were in favor of the dollar against the yen and the French franc, with a narrowing of the negative differential vis-à-vis the Italian lira (Charts 4, 9, and 10).

Further convergence of inflation rates has also contributed to the recent stability of exchange rates within the ERM. At end-1988 the inflation differential between France and Germany amounted to 1.4 percentage points and to 3.7 percentage points between Italy and Germany, in both cases the smallest since the early

Chart 9. Short-Term U.S. Dollar and Japanese Yen Interest Rates, 1984–90

(In percent per annum)

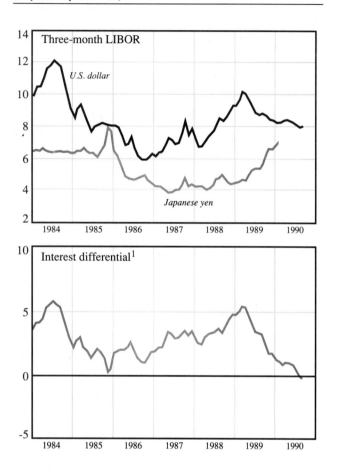

Source: International Monetary Fund, Data Fund.
[1] U.S. dollar rate minus Japanese yen rate.

Chart 10. Short-Term U.S. Dollar and Italian Lira Interest Rates, 1984–90

(In percent per annum)

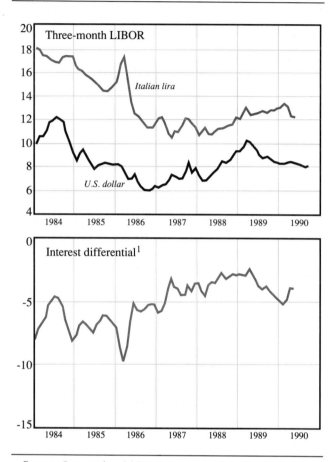

Source: International Monetary Fund, Data Fund.
[1] U.S. dollar rate minus Italian lira rate.

1970s and hence since the inception of the EMS.[34] If sustained, such gains in convergence (which extend to interest rates—see Charts 11 and 12) would seem to suggest that, ceteris paribus, future realignments, if necessary, would be smaller than in the past.

The weakening of the deutsche mark vis-à-vis the dollar (and other ERM currencies) seems to have stemmed at least in part from market reactions to the announcement of the introduction as of January 1, 1989 of a withholding tax on interest income in Germany[35] and from the substantial tightening of the monetary policy stance in the United Kingdom that pushed nomi-

nal interest rates to levels much higher than in the ERM countries (Chart 13).[36] The greater availability of direct investment opportunities in some of the faster-growing industrial economies outside the ERM may also have contributed to deutsche mark weakness.

On June 19, 1989, the Spanish peseta joined the exchange rate mechanism of the EMS with fluctuation margins of ± 6 percent. In the months following its entry the spread between strong and weak currencies within the band widened, reflecting strong upward pressures on the peseta—which reached its upper intervention limit in September—linked to large direct and portfolio investment inflows in a context of buoyant GDP growth and high domestic interest rates. Throughout much of 1989 the Spanish authorities tried

[34] In contrast, the inflation differential between the United Kingdom and Germany stood at 5.1 percentage points, well above the corresponding differential with respect to the EC and OECD averages.
[35] This tax was repealed on July 1, 1989.

[36] This hardening of the stance of monetary policy reflected concern about inflationary pressures, the rapid growth of wages, and a widening of the current account deficit.

Chart 11. Short-Term French Franc and Deutsche Mark Interest Rates, 1984–90

(In percent per annum)

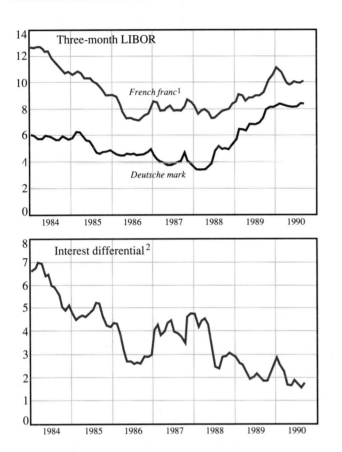

Chart 12. Short-Term Italian Lira and Deutsche Mark Interest Rates, 1984–90

(In percent per annum)

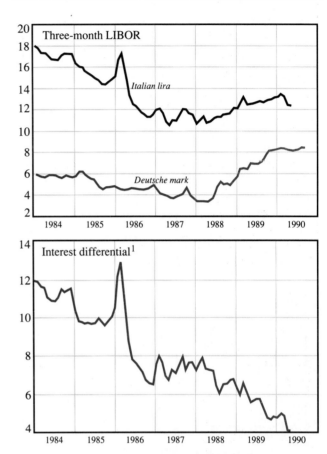

Source: International Monetary Fund, Data Fund.
[1] Interbank money rate.
[2] French franc rate minus deutsche mark rate.

Source: International Monetary Fund, Data Fund.
[1] Italian lira rate minus deutsche mark rate.

repeatedly to stem the growth of domestic demand, through both monetary and fiscal measures. Evidence suggests that these efforts are beginning to pay off: inflation appears to have leveled off, the growth of the main money and credit aggregates has subsided, and a number of indicators of private consumption indicate some cooling of the economy.

A noteworthy development during this period was the increasing resilience of the ERM, in the wake of the Basle/Nyborg agreement, to changes in the underlying conditions of individual currencies. The liberalization of exchange restrictions undertaken by the Italian authorities during 1988 was typical. The temporary controls on leads and lags in payments related to trade transactions imposed in September 1987 were lifted on

January 20, 1988.[37] Some of the liberalization measures that were to take effect on October 1, 1988 were advanced to June, including the virtual abolition of all restrictions on payments related to tourism. On October 1, 1988 a new foreign exchange law came into effect. It effectively removed most exchange restrictions on residents and extended the guarantee of free repatriation of capital and income to all types of investment. (As of May 14, 1990, all remaining controls were abolished.) Throughout this period of increased liberal-

[37] Outflows of speculative short-term capital, together with a worsening trade performance contributed to a large loss of international reserves in August and early September 1987. Monetary policy was tightened and complemented by a package of exchange control measures announced on September 13, 1987. The measures included the reimposition of a ceiling on commercial bank credit to the private sector and the tightening of controls on leads and lags relating to trade payments.

Chart 13. Short-Term Pound Sterling and Deutsche Mark Interest Rates, 1984–90

(In percent per annum)

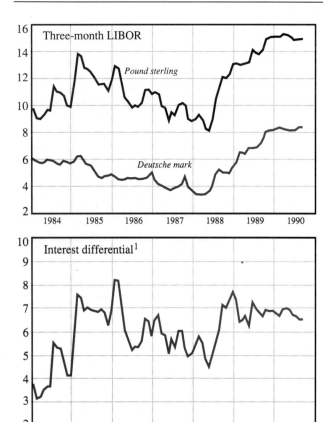

Source: International Monetary Fund, Data Fund.
[1] Pound sterling rate minus deutsche mark rate.

ization, exchange rate management in Italy relied exclusively on market mechanisms; in particular, pressures on the lira did not occur or were never sufficiently strong to make a realignment within the ERM necessary. Other episodes of stress within the ERM during this period—as in August/September 1988—were successfully dealt with through intervention (at times large scale), a more active use of the fluctuation margin, and improved coordination of interest rate policies.

The January 1990 Realignment and Other Developments

In what was described as "one of the smoothest realignments since the system began operating in March 1979," the Italian lira was devalued by 3.7 percent effective January 8, 1990. The Italian authorities'

request for a realignment was accompanied by their decision to place the lira in the narrow 2.25 percent fluctuation band of the ERM, ahead of the July 1, 1990 deadline for the liberalization of capital movements.[38] The new central rate for the lira was fixed at approximately its market rate with the result that its lower intervention limits remained unchanged, except for the Spanish peseta. The Italian authorities also pledged a renewed commitment to fiscal discipline aimed at maintaining the deficit within forecast limits and at encouraging a swifter reduction in inflation.

The realignment of the lira followed a period of significant strengthening of the deutsche mark in foreign exchange markets in the latter part of 1989, partly linked to political developments in Eastern Europe. Market perceptions of the potential gains to the Federal Republic of Germany as a result of liberalization in Eastern European countries attracted foreign investment inflows and at that stage exerted upward pressure on the deutsche mark. It appreciated by close to 10 percent against the dollar and the yen in the last two months of 1989, contributing to the emergence of tensions within the ERM. The devaluation of the lira was thus an attempt to accommodate the currency's downward move against the deutsche mark. Following the realignment, however, the lira moved to the top of the narrow band and remained there through the first half of 1990, while the other currencies in the narrow band clustered at the bottom of the band.

As mentioned above, the pound sterling joined the ERM as of October 8, 1990 with the use of the wider margins of ± 6 percent. This move is expected to reduce fluctuations of sterling against other ERM currencies and to assist in lowering inflation. Effective October 22, 1990, the Norwegian krone was pegged to the ECU, with fluctuation margins of ± 2.25 percent.

Exchange Rate Variability

In discussing exchange rate movements, it is useful to distinguish between misalignments—long-term movements of exchange rates away from an underlying exchange rate that would establish external balance in general equilibrium—and variability (or volatility)—short-term movements around an expected exchange

---

[38] Following the inclusion of the peseta in the ERM, movements of the currencies in the wider band vis-à-vis those in the narrow band were constrained by a limitation of ± 6 percent on cross-rates between currencies in the wider band. It was thus no coincidence that during periods when the peseta was close to its upper intervention limit (early September 1989), the lira remained close to the currencies of the narrow band. This de facto constraint on the lira is thought to have been a factor in the authorities' decision to move the lira into the narrow band.

rate level or trend.[39] The existence of possible exchange rate misalignments in the ERM are discussed below, while the focus here is on exchange rate variability.

Exchange rate variability is generally regarded as undesirable when it increases the payment risks associated with international trade. This would happen when transactions between two parties take place at exchange rates that are different from those expected by either party at the time the transactions were planned or agreed. Traders averse to risk would then reduce the level of international exchange and engage in safer, albeit less productive, activities, and hence, economic welfare would decline. So far, it has remained an open empirical question whether exchange rate variability actually has the presumed negative effects.[40] But this question has not prevented politicians from seeking to achieve greater exchange rate stability.

In principle, payment risks associated with exchange rate variability can be reduced by selling or buying the currency involved in an international transaction in the forward market. If everybody engaging in international transactions had unrestricted and immediate access to a well-functioning forward market for currencies (giving unbiased predictions of future spot rates), exchange rate variability would not have to be an economic policy issue. In reality, however, access to forward markets is limited and, particularly for small companies and individuals, is often associated with relatively high transaction costs. Consequently, exchange rate variability has been considered particularly undesirable in very open economies in which many small companies and individuals with limited access to forward markets engage in international exchanges. Given the intense trade relations between EC countries, an important reason for the establishment of the EMS was therefore its expected positive effect on exchange rate stability between those currencies that were to participate in the ERM. The degree to which these expectations have been fulfilled is regarded as an important criterion for the success of the system.

An assessment of the effects of the ERM on the exchange rate variability of ERM currencies—defined as short-term exchange rate movements around an expected exchange rate level or trend—cannot be judged independently. In particular, measurement of exchange rate variability makes it necessary to define a reference level from which actual deviations of exchange rates are calculated. Since expected exchange rates cannot be observed—given limited market access, forward rates may not reflect the expectations of all individuals engaged in international exchanges—some plausible reference levels have to be assumed. Moreover, assessment of the contribution of the ERM to exchange rate stability would in principle require estimating counterfactual exchange rate developments (that is, of exchange rate movements in the absence of the ERM). Given the technical difficulties associated with such an undertaking, simpler techniques, such as comparing exchange rate variability before and after the inception of the EMS or for the currencies of ERM and non-ERM countries, have to be employed.

Despite these technical and methodological difficulties, the numerous studies conducted on this issue have generally concluded that variability of nominal and real exchange rates of ERM currencies against their partner currencies has declined since the establishment of the EMS.[41] This study confirms this finding by extending the observation period through 1989 (Tables 10 and 11).[42] Variability of bilateral nominal exchange rates of ERM countries against their partners declined substantially, on average, between 1974–78 and 1979–89, irrespective of the method of measurement (Table 10). The trend toward lower variability was most pronounced in the more recent years, reflecting the absence of a realignment of central rates in the ERM between January 1987 and January 1990. Nominal exchange rate variability for the group of non-ERM countries hardly changed between 1974–78 and 1979–89 as the substantial decline in variability of currencies of European non-ERM countries (some of which, notably Austria, have in fact become shadow participants in the ERM) was offset by an increase in variability of currencies of other countries. But variability of bilateral nominal exchange rates of ERM currencies against non-ERM currencies increased considerably on average between the two time periods, while that of bilateral rates between non-ERM currencies increased much less. A decline in variability of both groups occurred, however, after 1986, reflecting efforts by the Group of Seven countries toward greater exchange rate stability in the context of the Plaza Agreement of September 1985 and the Louvre Accord of February 1987 (see above).

The pattern of changes in exchange rate variability between 1974–78 and 1979–89 is not much different for

---

[39] See Williamson (1983).
[40] For a discussion of this issue, see International Monetary Fund (1984). For a recent empirical study, see Caballero and Corbo (1989).

[41] See, for example, Guitián (1988) and the literature quoted there. See also Artis and Taylor (1989).
[42] In this study exchange rate variability is defined either as the coefficient of variation of monthly exchange rates or as the standard deviation of the monthly changes in the natural logarithm of exchange rates in a year. The first concept of measurement appears more appropriate if the stable, or expected, exchange rates remain unchanged while the second concept appears to apply when the stable, or expected, exchange rates follow a trend.

ERM countries, when real (consumer price-adjusted) bilateral exchange rates are considered reflecting the considerable inflation convergence that has been achieved in these countries during the ERM period (Table 11). For non-ERM countries, real exchange rate variability on average changed only little or increased. Thus, one may conclude that the objective of greater exchange rate stability within the ERM currency area has been achieved both in absolute as well as in relative (to the non-ERM currencies) terms.

But the sharp decline in nominal and real bilateral exchange rate variability of ERM currencies against partner currencies, together with the increase against the group of non-ERM currencies, has resulted in only a moderate decline in the variability of the nominal and real effective exchange rates of ERM countries between 1975–78 and 1979–89 (Table 12). Interestingly, despite relatively small changes or increases in the variability of bilateral nominal and real exchange rates of non-ERM countries, there has been a decline in the variability of nominal and real effective exchange rates of the non-ERM countries. This result suggests that the covariance between the component currencies of the effective exchange rate indexes of non-ERM countries was on average greater during 1975–78 than during 1979–89.[43] This result may have been due, in part, to the strong inverse movements of the dollar relative to the ERM currencies during the ERM period.

Economic Convergence Among EMS Member Countries

Conceptual Considerations

In general terms, economic convergence can be defined as the narrowing of differences in the development of economic (target and policy) variables. In a particular case, it is, of course, necessary to specify which set of variables is to converge. In referring to the ultimate objective of an economically fully integrated EC, economic convergence has been identified with the improvement and convergence of living and working conditions in EC member countries.[44] In the EMS context, on the other hand, economic convergence has been considered necessary to establish a

sound basis for stable exchange rates among EMS member countries. To avoid confusion, it is therefore useful to distinguish between the ultimate goal of convergence in living and working conditions—occasionally referred to as "real" convergence—and the objective of stable exchange rates, which is often considered an intermediate objective on the way to the ultimate goal. The attainment of stable exchange rates is believed to require convergence of a specific set of economic variables such as costs and prices; this has been referred to as nominal convergence.[45]

Convergence of the development of costs and prices in the traded and nontraded goods sectors is generally regarded as a necessary condition for a stable nominal exchange rate between two countries.[46] Possible differences in price inflation in the traded goods sector are presumed to disturb the external equilibrium between the two countries with the low-inflation country gaining domestic and foreign market shares at the expense of the high-inflation country. If the law of one price prevails in the traded goods sector, differences in cost inflation are seen to lead to differences in profitability in the traded goods sector with similar consequences for market shares of the high- and low-cost countries. Divergences between countries in the price developments of nontraded goods are believed to signal differences in incentives for resource reallocation to the nontraded goods sector that have implications for market shares in tradables and therefore for external equilibrium.

Widely used indicators of cost and price performance are unit labor costs in manufacturing, aggregate consumer prices, and GNP deflators. While the latter two measures combine the prices of traded and nontraded goods, it is not considered to be a disadvantage. Even if there were price and cost convergence in the traded goods sector (indicated by the parallel development of unit labor costs in this sector), divergent developments of the aggregate prices could indicate shifts of resources to the nontraded goods sector of different magnitude. Although in the following the usual price and cost indicators are used to assess to what extent the necessary conditions for exchange rate stability in the ERM have been fulfilled, it should be noted that conventional interpretations, as given above, are based upon a number of fairly restrictive assumptions.[47]

---

[43] The variance of a composite such as an effective exchange rate index is given by the (weighted) sum of the variances and the covariances of the components. Thus, if the components of the index are positively (negatively) correlated, the variance of the index will be greater (less) than the (weighted) sum of the variances of the components.

[44] See Preamble to the Treaty establishing the European Economic Community.

[45] See Commission of the European Communities (1989b). For a further discussion of the concept of convergence see Ungerer, Evans, and Nyberg (1983), p. 10.

[46] Once convergence is achieved, nominal exchange rates can be adjusted to reflect relative costs and prices.

[47] Specifically, for unit labor costs to measure competitiveness in one country relative to another appropriately, it must be assumed that (i) the development of input costs other than labor is broadly the same; (ii) the countries under consideration share a similar production technology; (iii) the structure of demand

Convergence of costs and prices has often been regarded as a necessary but insufficient condition for exchange rate stability. For example, even if prices and costs of two countries were to converge temporarily, emerging differences in the respective stance of macroeconomic policies could cause renewed divergence or lead to external disequilibrium that in turn could put pressure on exchange rates. Thus, in the absence of exogenous shocks affecting countries differently, convergence of the stance of macroeconomic policies has been regarded as an additional prerequisite for exchange rate stability.

Regarding monetary policy, there has been broad agreement that it should aim at reducing differences in rates of inflation and thereby stabilize exchange rates. This result could be achieved in two ways. ERM countries could either agree on a common rate of inflation, establish a common monetary target, and derive from this target national targets for monetary policy, or one ERM country could establish the ERM rate of inflation by following an independent monetary policy while others peg their exchange rate to the currency of that country and allow their monetary policy to be determined by the exchange rate link. Although adjustment of both high- and low-inflation countries to some common rate of inflation was initially regarded as an option, the view eventually gained strength that the country with the lowest rate of inflation should set the standard toward which the other countries should converge.[48] In practice, this view implied that the ERM gravitated toward the deutsche mark as the nominal anchor of the system. Reflecting its mandate, the Bundesbank concentrated on maintaining the internal purchasing power for the deutsche mark while other member countries followed policies that minimized the size and frequency of devaluations of their currencies vis-à-vis the deutsche mark. In this case, stable exchange rates would be compatible with monetary expansion in the follower countries in line with monetary expansion in the anchor country adjusted for real growth differences and exogenous differences in changes in velocity.

In fiscal policy, the implications of stable exchange rates are less clear. In principle, with monetary policy geared toward stabilizing the exchange rate and reducing inflation differentials, fiscal policy could attempt to pursue domestic objectives (for example, lowering unemployment). The resulting stance of fiscal policy may, however, not be compatible with the prevailing exchange rate and may require offsetting action by monetary policy. Depending on the circumstances, this action could endanger price stability, growth, or external equilibrium. It has therefore been argued that exchange rate stability would be supported by the convergence of government deficits among ERM countries.[49]

In the following, empirical evidence is presented on the record in ("nominal") economic convergence among the original ERM countries during the ERM period and the role of policies therein.[50] Developments in ERM countries are then compared with those in a group of selected non-ERM countries, comprising the major industrial countries.

External Balances

The above considerations suggest that divergences in cost and price performance and/or in the stance of macroeconomic policies may contribute to external imbalances among ERM countries if their effects are not offset by exchange rate adjustments. Developments in overall external current account and trade balances as well as trade balances vis-à-vis ERM partners and other countries are presented in Tables 13–16. Altogether, external current account and trade imbalances relative to GNP diminished on average for the group of ERM countries through the 1980s, while there was no marked increase in the differences in external economic performance from the four years preceding the inception of the ERM. External imbalances of a group of selected non-ERM industrial countries[51] on the other hand, after narrowing in the mid-1980s, widened again more recently and differences in performance remained large.

After higher average deficits relative to GDP/GNP in the aftermath of the second oil price shock in 1979, the

---

remains basically unchanged in both countries; and (iv) the focus is on short-run developments. For aggregate price indices to be meaningful indicators, it has to be assumed in addition that productivity growth in the nontraded goods sector in the countries under consideration is similar. Since these assumptions may not always be fulfilled, international divergences in the development of the traditional price and cost indicators do not in all cases imply that exchange rate stability is endangered. See Lipschitz and McDonald (1990) for a detailed discussion of these issues.

[48] In the early 1980s, there was a general consensus among policymakers in Europe and elsewhere that inflation had to be brought down. In this situation, monetary policies that would have left it to the majority of member countries to determine the Community price level on an average basis were seen as suboptimal, particularly when many of these countries had domestic political problems in keeping inflation under control.

[49] Whether convergence of deficits would be brought about by market forces or require coordination of fiscal policies is another, hotly debated issue. See Section V for a review of the different arguments.

[50] Since Spain and the United Kingdom joined the ERM only in June 1989 and October 1990, respectively, they are classified as non-ERM countries in the discussion of developments that took place during the first decade of the ERM.

[51] Austria, Norway, Spain, Sweden, Switzerland, and the United Kingdom were selected as European comparator countries. Australia, Canada, Japan, and the United States were chosen as non-European comparator countries.

external current accounts of ERM countries improved through the 1980s and eventually became stronger than during the second half of the 1970s (Table 13). Parallel to this development, divergences in current account performance among ERM countries, after having increased during the time of current account deterioration in absolute terms (measured in terms of standard deviation from the group mean), narrowed again in more recent years. This reflected improvements in the external current account positions of all ERM countries from the levels recorded in the early 1980s. Average external current account deficits relative to GDP/GNP in the group of non-ERM countries, however, deteriorated during the second half of the 1980s, after an improvement during the second half of the 1970s and the first half of the 1980s. The divergence in current account performance among this group, after a temporary decline in 1979–82, remained high through the 1980s.[52]

Although differences in overall external economic performance relative to GNP may not have increased markedly among ERM countries during the first decade of the ERM, the capital flows needed for the financing of these differences have. The external current account position of the largest ERM economy, the Federal Republic of Germany, improved by 5 percent of GNP (or $58.5 billion) between 1979–82 and 1989. Similarly, in the group of non-ERM countries, the external current account balance of the largest economy, the United States, deteriorated by about 2½ percent of GNP ($125 billion) between 1979–82 and 1989, while that of the second largest, Japan, improved by a similar amount relative to GNP ($74 billion). Thus, the aggregate external current account surplus of the group of ERM countries rose by $67.5 billion during this period while that of non-ERM countries deteriorated by $115 billion, giving rise to unprecedented capital flows between and within the two groups (Table 15).

The developments of aggregate external balances presented in Tables 13 and 14 hide the increase in regional imbalances that have occurred in the ERM during more recent years. In particular, Germany's external trade surplus with its ERM partner countries increased from $2.2 billion to $26.3 billion from the four-year period preceding inception of the ERM to 1988, while the combined deficit of France and Italy rose from $3.4 billion to $25.7 billion (Table 16). Differences in internal ERM trade performance between these countries have increased in recent years as Germany's surplus vis-à-vis ERM partner countries more than quadrupled between 1983–86 and 1989 while its surplus with other countries only doubled. France's deficit with its ERM partners rose by more than half in this period while it accumulated substantial surpluses with other countries, and Italy's deficit with the ERM more than doubled while its trade balance with other countries sharply improved. The emergence of large external imbalances among ERM countries during a period of increasing nominal exchange rate stability in the ERM has raised concerns about insufficient convergence of cost and price developments and differences in the stance of policies, in particular of fiscal policy.[53] These issues will be taken up below.

Prices and Costs

As noted above, convergence of prices and costs is generally seen as a necessary condition to sustain exchange rate stability. To the extent that convergence is insufficient and exchange rates are rigid, external current account imbalances, as they have emerged in the ERM in recent years, are likely. Rates of price and labor cost inflation in ERM and other countries before and during the ERM period are presented in Tables 17–20. In general, there has been a strong trend toward both lower average price and labor cost inflation and toward a higher degree of convergence in ERM countries.

After remaining broadly unchanged on average in 1979–82 from the four-year period preceding the ERM, the ERM average rate of consumer price inflation came down sharply in the following years but increased again somewhat in 1989 (Table 17). Also, inflation convergence improved considerably during the ERM period (Chart 14 and Table 17). Discussion has been lively, mainly among academics, on whether participation in the ERM was instrumental in the decline of inflation in ERM countries or whether this decline only reflected a general trend toward lower inflation in the world at large. It may be impossible to settle this question on the basis of empirical tests to the satisfaction of all the

---

[52] Average trade balances relative to GNP for the group of ERM countries recorded a larger improvement through the 1980s than external current account balances, owing mainly to a very sharp rise in the trade surplus of Ireland (Table 14). Reflecting the extraordinary improvement of the Irish trade balance, the divergence in external trade positions among ERM countries increased in absolute terms through the 1980s, but declined somewhat in relative terms (measured by standard deviations corrected for movements of means or coefficients of variation). In the group of non-ERM countries, average relative trade balances deteriorated through the 1980s, while differences in trade performance remained high.

[53] On the other hand, the emergence of large external imbalances has been regarded as an indication of greater capital mobility among ERM countries and therefore as of little concern to policymakers.

Chart 14. ERM: Maximum and Minimum Rates of Inflation

(Consumer price indices)

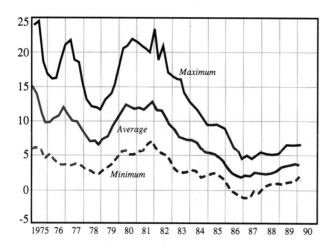

Source: International Monetary Fund, *International Financial Statistics*.

parties involved.[54] It is nevertheless worth noting that while inflation decelerated also in other countries, the deceleration in a number of ERM countries was sharper than elsewhere. As a result, average inflation in the ERM fell more between 1975–78 and 1989 and was lower than in the group of selected non-ERM countries. Disinflation in the non-ERM country group was still somewhat smaller even if the non-European countries are excluded (Table 17). These patterns are not changed if GNP deflators are used instead of consumer prices as inflation indicators (Table 18).

Coinciding with the process of price disinflation, there has been a considerable decline in average wage inflation, and an increase in the convergence of national wage inflation, in the ERM as well as in the selected non-ERM countries through the 1980s (Table 19). With productivity increases in ERM countries considerably exceeding wage inflation, the deceleration of unit labor cost increases was sharper than that of wage inflation; it was also sharper in ERM countries than in the group of non-ERM countries (Table 20). Convergence in unit

[54] While Collins (1988) did not find evidence of any shift in inflation behavior of ERM countries after 1979, Russo and Tullio (1988) and, more recently, Chowdhury and Sdogati (1990) came to the conclusion that ERM commitments played a positive role in bringing down inflation. See also Giavazzi and Giovannini (1988) and Harbrecht and Schmid (1988). On the question whether the EMS is providing a policy and operational framework for a credible disinflation strategy, see Thygesen (1988) and Rey (1988). For a detailed analysis of the process of disinflation in Italy and Ireland, see Gressani, Guiso, and Visco (1988) and Kremers (1990), respectively.

labor cost inflation among ERM participants increased in absolute terms (measured by standard deviations), but it decreased in relative terms (measured by standard deviations relative to the group mean).[55]

External Competitiveness

Although price and cost inflation has converged among ERM countries through the ERM period, remaining divergences that were not offset by exchange rate adjustments could have led to shifts in competitiveness and thereby to an increase in external imbalances among ERM countries. The probability of a shift in competitiveness would be increased to the extent that those countries in the ERM that had suffered from relatively high inflation rates during the second part of the 1970s and in the early 1980s have used the exchange rate as an instrument to disinflate. By devaluing their currency by less than the cost-price differential vis-à-vis the anchor currency of the system, it has been argued, these countries have made use of the ERM to import price stability, but at the cost of an erosion of competitiveness against their partners.[56]

Charts 15–17 show the developments of indices for consumer prices, unit labor costs, and value-added deflators (both in manufacturing), adjusted for exchange rate changes of six ERM countries relative to the Federal Republic of Germany, the anchor country for the system. Chart 15 illustrates that only in

[55] However, divergence measured by coefficients of variation is overstated when the sample mean approaches zero.

[56] These countries are seen to have drifted away from the level of competitiveness that they had attained when they joined the ERM. See Melitz (1988).

Chart 15. ERM: Consumer Price Index Relative to Federal Republic of Germany

(Adjusted for exchange rate changes; 1979 I = 100)

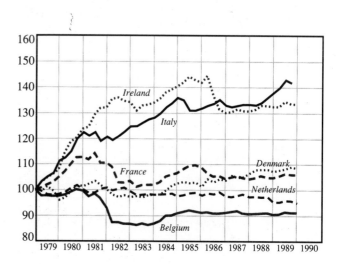

Ireland and Italy did relative consumer prices adjusted for exchange rate changes increase considerably above the levels prevailing at the inception of the system. In Ireland, relative adjusted consumer prices increased substantially until the middle of 1986. After the devaluation of the Irish pound on August 4, 1986, they dropped; a further decline in early 1987 reflected the revaluation of the deutsche mark in the realignment of January 12, 1987. Since then, relative adjusted consumer prices have increased again, but much slower than in earlier years. In Italy, after a steep increase until the first half of 1985, relative adjusted consumer prices were broadly stable until the end of 1988; they increased rapidly again during the first three quarters of 1989. France reversed part of an initial increase in relative adjusted consumer prices, while Denmark, after broadly stable prices, has experienced an increase since early 1984. In Belgium and the Netherlands, relative adjusted consumer prices either fell or changed little.

Relative adjusted unit labor costs in manufacturing decreased in Belgium, Denmark, and the Netherlands through the ERM period; after an initial increase, they also fell in France and Ireland below the levels attained at the beginning of the ERM period (Chart 16). In Italy, however, a sharp increase during 1979–84 was only partly offset in 1985–88, and reversed in 1989. Developments in relative adjusted value-added deflators in manufacturing were similar to those in unit labor costs (Chart 17).[57]

---

[57] In Italy, relative adjusted consumer prices increased more than relative adjusted unit labor costs and value-added deflators in manufacturing, which may reflect a sharper rise in the relative price of nontradables in this country than in Germany.

Chart 16. ERM: Normalized Unit Labor Costs Relative to Federal Republic of Germany

(Adjusted for exchange rate changes; 1979 I = 100)

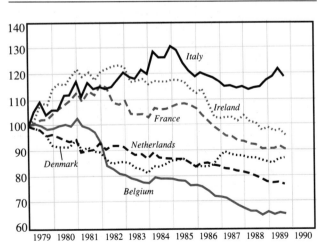

Chart 17. ERM: Value-Added Deflator Relative to Federal Republic of Germany

(Adjusted for exchange rate changes; 1979 I = 100)

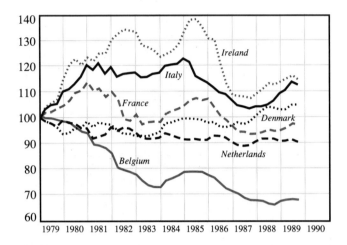

Changes in consumer prices, unit labor costs, and value-added deflators of ERM countries, adjusted for exchange rate changes relative to each of their partners since the inception of the ERM, are presented in Tables 21–23; the trade-weighted averages of these indicators for each ERM country relative to the group of its partner countries—and an indicator of relative profitability in manufacturing[58]—are plotted in Charts 18–24. Regardless of the indicator considered, Belgium's external competitiveness vis-à-vis its ERM partners appears to have improved throughout the ERM period, whereas in Denmark initial improvements in relative consumer prices and unit labor costs were subsequently eroded; the increase in the relative value-added deflator parallel to relative unit labor costs indicates that Danish producers preferred to accept losses in market shares—and a deterioration of the external accounts—than a decline in profitability. In France, most of the indicators point to a broadly stable level of competitiveness. In the Federal Republic of Germany, both relative unit labor costs and value-added deflators (and, by implication, relative profitability) suggest a deterioration of external competitiveness against ERM partners while relative consumer prices, after an initial improvement, have remained stable. In Ireland, competitiveness appears to have improved more recently after some deterioration in the early 1980s, while in

---

[58] Profitability is measured by the ratio of value-added deflators to unit labor costs. An increase in unit labor costs with unchanged value-added deflators indicates a profit squeeze, reflected in a drop in the profitability indicator.

Chart 18. Belgium: Indicators of Competitiveness Relative to ERM Partners

(1979 I = 100)

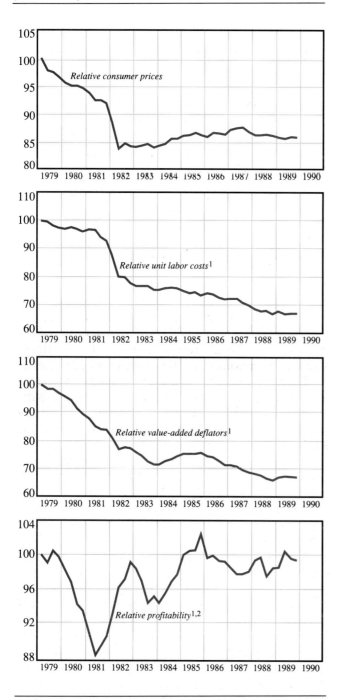

Chart 19. Denmark: Indicators of Competitiveness Relative to ERM Partners

(1979 I = 100)

Source: International Monetary Fund, *International Financial Statistics*.

[1] In manufacturing.

[2] Relative value-added deflator divided by relative unit labor costs.

Source: International Monetary Fund, *International Financial Statistics*.

[1] In manufacturing.

[2] Relative value-added deflator divided by relative unit labor costs.

Chart 20. France: Indicators of Competitiveness Relative to ERM Partners

(1979 I = 100)

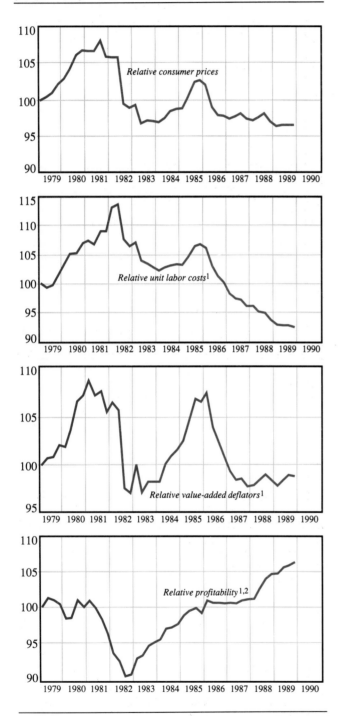

Source: International Monetary Fund, *International Financial Statistics*.
[1] In manufacturing.
[2] Relative value-added deflator divided by relative unit labor costs.

Chart 21. Federal Republic of Germany: Indicators of Competitiveness Relative to ERM Partners

(1979 I = 100)

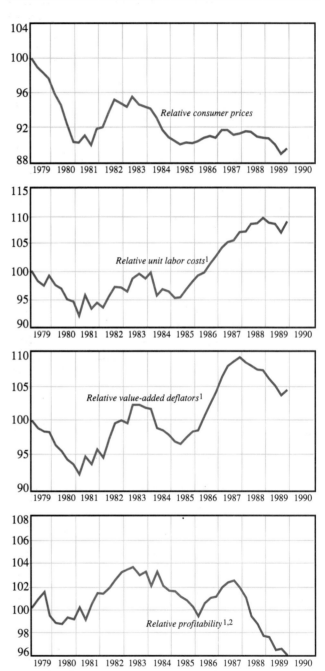

Source: International Monetary Fund, *International Financial Statistics*.
[1] In manufacturing.
[2] Relative value-added deflator divided by relative unit labor costs.

Chart 22. Ireland: Indicators of Competitiveness Relative to ERM Partners

(1979 I = 100)

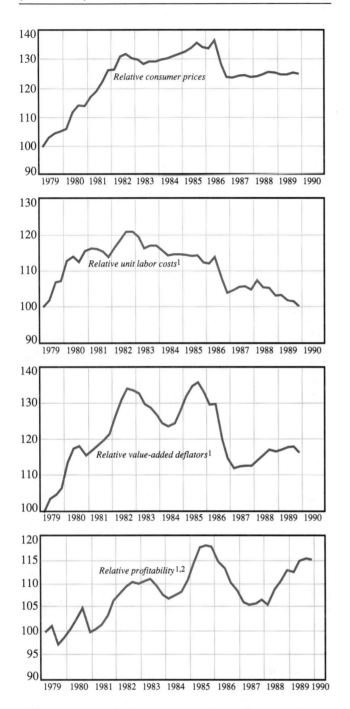

Chart 23. Italy: Indicators of Competitiveness Relative to ERM Partners

(1979 I = 100)

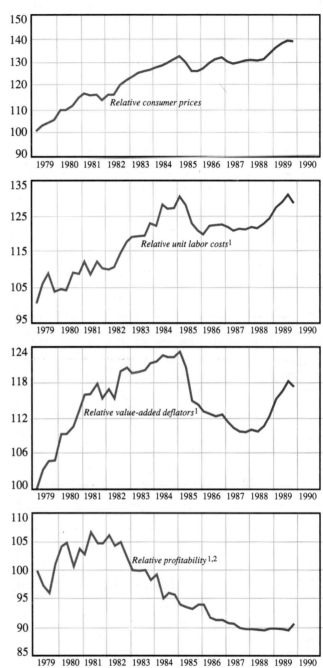

Source: International Monetary Fund, *International Financial Statistics*.
[1] In manufacturing.
[2] Relative value-added deflator divided by relative unit labor costs.

Source: International Monetary Fund, *International Financial Statistics*.
[1] In manufacturing.
[2] Relative value-added deflator divided by relative unit labor costs.

Chart 24. Netherlands: Indicators of Competitiveness Relative to ERM Partners

(1979 I = 100)

Relative consumer prices

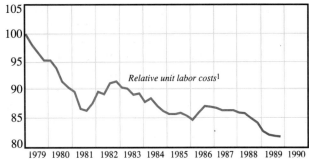

Relative unit labor costs[1]

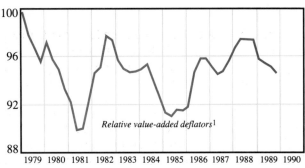

Relative value-added deflators[1]

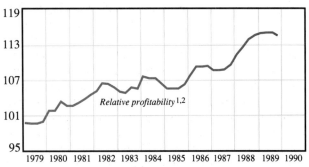

Relative profitability[1,2]

Source: International Monetary Fund, *International Financial Statistics*.

[1] In manufacturing.

[2] Relative value-added deflator divided by relative unit labor costs.

Italy, after a similar development through 1988, competitiveness appears to have deteriorated again since the end of that year. In the Netherlands, competitiveness has on balance improved during the ERM period.

Table 24 shows real effective exchange rates based on unit labor costs of ERM and other countries relative to the German rate. On average, Germany's ERM partners have been able to improve their competitiveness relative to Germany through the 1980s, while that of non-ERM countries has remained broadly stable. Within the ERM, however, Italy has lost competitiveness relative to Germany.

The indicators considered in this section suggest that there has been no systematic shift in competitiveness among most ERM countries during the ERM period, and, therefore, no major misalignments of exchange rates appear to have occurred. But it seems that some countries (Denmark and Italy) have suffered an erosion in their external competitiveness that could have contributed to their external deficits.[59]

Monetary Policy

As mentioned above, without exchange rate pressures elsewhere in the economy, stable exchange rates of ERM currencies vis-à-vis the anchor currency of the system, the deutsche mark, would be compatible with monetary expansion in the follower countries in line with monetary expansion in the anchor country, adjusted for real growth differences and exogenous changes in velocity (that is, changes in velocity not related to the stance of monetary policy). To the extent that divergences in the latter two variables were relatively small, some convergence of monetary aggregates should have occurred during the ERM period. Table 26, however, indicates that considerable divergences in the expansion of broad money have persisted through most of the ERM period, although average monetary expansion has slowed considerably in line with disinflation. Only in 1988 does there seem to have been stronger convergence in money growth. With increased convergence in rates of price inflation and relatively small differences in real growth rates among ERM countries, these divergences reflected considerable differences in the development of velocity (Table 27). Although institutional changes in the monetary sectors of ERM countries could have contributed to different

[59] Evidence gleaned from export market share data provides support for these main conclusions (Table 25). The loss of export market shares for some of these countries can, however, be attributed to many factors, including changes in real exchange rates, shifts in the patterns of world trade flows, differences in output growth, and in certain nonprice aspects of competitiveness, with the share of newly industrializing countries in world trade generally rising. Also, the sharp depreciation of the dollar after 1985 substantially improved the competitive position of non-oil exporting countries with dollar-based currencies.

developments of velocity, the size of the variations point to differences in the stance of monetary policy among ERM countries, which may have been facilitated by the presence of restrictions on international capital flows. In this regard, it is interesting to note that convergence in monetary expansion improved considerably in 1988, the year when agreement was reached in the EC to abolish by mid-1990 the remaining capital controls in most ERM countries.[60]

Divergences in the stance of monetary policy among ERM countries, as suggested by differences in the development of velocity, if indeed existent, should have been associated with divergences in the development of interest rates. As indicated in Table 28, correlation of short-term interest rates in ERM countries with rates in Germany, the anchor country, have been weaker in most countries than would have been expected with a high degree of monetary convergence. In particular, correlations have been low since the beginning of 1987, suggesting that interest rate differentials have been used as an instrument to stabilize exchange rates within the ERM. In Denmark and Ireland rates moved inversely to German rates during that period, but correlation with Germany was also relatively weak in Belgium and France. In the Netherlands and Italy, on the other hand, correlation of short-term rates with German rates has been high throughout the ERM period. However, correlations of long-term rates have at times been different from those of short-term rates, perhaps indicating different degrees of confidence in countries' monetary policies. In particular, correlations were high in Belgium and the Netherlands during the ERM period, indicating a high degree of convergence of inflationary expectations with Germany and, consequently, stable exchange rate expectations, but correlations were relatively low in the other countries, especially since 1987 (Table 29).

If interest rates have been used to stabilize exchange rates despite pressures for change, there is the possibility that exchange rate stability could have been achieved at the cost of interest rate stability.[61] There is, however, little empirical evidence for this. As indicated in Table 30, variability of short-term rates has in general been less during the ERM period than during the four years preceding the ERM. Variability of long-

term rates, however, increased substantially in most countries in 1979–86, but declined again thereafter.

Fiscal Policy

With the objective of exchange rate stability gaining importance in many ERM countries in recent years, the observed divergences in the stance of monetary policy may well have been necessary to compensate for wide and persistent divergences in fiscal policy. As Table 31 indicates, high average general government budget deficits in ERM countries were accompanied by large differences in fiscal performance among them, with Italy running double-digit deficits relative to GNP throughout the ERM period and Denmark running considerable surpluses in 1986–87. These two countries seem to have followed opposite policy mixes: Denmark in the mid-1980s tended to combine a more restrictive fiscal policy with an expansionary monetary policy while Italy has adopted a tight monetary policy in view of persistent and high fiscal deficits. Both countries, however, have been losing international competitiveness and incurring external deficits vis-à-vis their partners during the ERM period (see above).

Conclusion

Although progress has been made toward greater convergence among ERM countries in some areas important for attaining exchange rate stability, neither the necessary (convergence of costs and prices) nor the necessary and sufficient conditions (convergence of costs, prices, and policies) for irrevocably fixed exchange rates among all ERM participants have been fulfilled.[62] A core group of ERM participants, including the Benelux countries, France, and Germany, has emerged, which appears to have achieved a high degree of convergence in the area of prices and costs consistent with a high degree of exchange rate stability. Regarding the other ERM countries, both Denmark and Italy were losing international competitiveness during the earlier years of the ERM and again more recently. In Ireland, after initial heavy losses, the decline in external competitiveness seems to have been contained in recent years, and the external position appears to have been consolidated primarily through a restrictive macroeconomic policy stance.

[60] The deadline for Ireland and Spain and for Greece and Portugal, however, has been set at end-1992; for details see Section IV.
[61] See, for example, Rogoff (1985).
[62] See also the assessment of economic convergence in the EC by the Commission of the European Communities (1989b).

IV Financial Integration in the European Community

The Internal Market Program and Financial Integration

Despite its visionary outlook to "an ever closer union among the peoples of Europe" (Preamble) and its far-reaching implications for the future, the EEC Treaty of 1957 adhered to a pragmatic, stepwise approach to integration. Much of the initial emphasis was on the completion of a common market in merchandise trade and on the related adoption of a joint trade policy vis-à-vis the rest of the world. The Treaty recognized the need to extend the common market to trade in services, and it called on members to liberalize capital movements "to the extent necessary to ensure the proper functioning of the common market" (Art. 67). The Treaty also contained safeguard clauses, in Article 73, for situations involving disturbances in financial markets and, in Article 108, in the case of balance of payments difficulties. In such circumstances members may temporarily resort to certain capital controls.

In practice, integration in the financial area progressed at a modest pace. In the early 1960s, EC member countries agreed (under two directives) to liberalize their controls over direct investments, short- and medium-term trade credits, and trade of quoted securities.[63] However, short-term capital movements not related to trade were excluded from liberalization, and other important differences in the treatment of capital movements remained. Some member countries had already liberalized broader categories of financial transactions, while others maintained a variety of restrictions that they sought to liberalize gradually. In 1968–73, a succession of international currency crises culminated in the breakdown of the Bretton Woods system. During this period of turbulence, several EC countries reverted to or intensified capital controls. Subsequently, the gradual liberalization of capital movements resumed.

Some progress toward integration and competition in the financial services markets was achieved as a result of the adoption of the First Banking Directive of 1977.[64] But the "southern expansion" of the EC, with Greece joining in 1981 and Spain and Portugal in 1986, broadened the range of institutional and structural differences within the EC, also with respect to the degree of capital liberalization and the integration of financial markets. Consequently, financial integration became more complicated.

In 1983, the EC Commission sent a "Communication on Financial Integration" to the Council of Ministers. This document, and the subsequent discussions, contributed to the key conclusion that the full liberalization of capital movements, the integration of financial services, and the reinforcement of the EMS were preconditions for the achievement of a fully unified market in the EC. In 1984 the EC Commission tightened the standards according to which countries could take exception from the agreed liberalization obligations. Such derogations were thereafter granted in fewer cases, and their scope and duration were more limited than previously.

In February 1986, the EC Council of Ministers adopted the Single European Act, which was ratified in 1987.[65] Its most important objective was the implementation of the comprehensive internal market program by the end of 1992. Moreover, it aimed at streamlining and democratizing decision making in the Community by introducing majority voting (instead of unanimity) in most areas of EC legislation, and it strengthened the role of the European Parliament. The Single Act also anchored in the EEC Treaty (Article 102A) the principle of economic and monetary cooperation and the need for convergence of economic and monetary policies. The legal and formal prerequisites of the internal market program were specified in a White Paper from the EC Commission to the European Council.[66] Given the complexities of the program, the

---

[63] OJ, No. 43, July 12, 1960, and OJ, No. 9, January 22, 1963.

[64] Council Directive 77/780/EEC of December 12, 1977, OJ, L 322, December 17, 1977.

[65] *Bulletin of the European Communities* (Brussels), Supplement 2/86.

[66] "Completing the Internal Market" (Brussels), COM (85) 310 final, June 1985.

Commission proposed that, in addition to the Community's established reliance on the principles of subsidiarity and harmonization, the principle of mutual recognition of administrative norms, usages, and requirements should be more extensively relied upon in the integration of trade in goods and services, including financial services.[67] Adoption of the principle of mutual recognition in such a broader role facilitated the preparatory work for the internal market.

In May 1986, the EC Commission proposed a timetable for the liberalization of capital movements that underlined the importance of full capital liberalization for further convergence of policies and performance within the EMS. Following the realignment of central rates within the ERM in January 1987, discussions within the EC further emphasized the link between the strengthening of the EMS and the full liberalization of capital movements. Measures designed to strengthen the EMS were adopted in September 1987 (see Section II). In November 1987, the EC Commission presented to the EC Council of Ministers comprehensive proposals to liberalize capital movements. These proposals served as the basis for further debate and for the new directive on liberalization of capital movements, which was adopted by the Council of Ministers on June 24, 1988.[68]

The Single European Act recognized that, in addition to full liberalization of capital movements, a sufficient liberalization and harmonization of the national laws governing the authorization of credit institutions and the provision of financial services constituted equally essential conditions for the completion of the internal market. The Second Banking Directive,[69] proposed in March 1988 and adopted in December 1989, is the main guideline in the EC's pursuit of codification and coordination in this area. It is supplemented in the prudential regulation area by the Solvency Ratio Directive,[70] the Directive on Credit Institutions' Own Funds,[71] and a proposed directive tightening the rules of risk exposures of banks. The strengthening of prudential requirements applicable to credit institutions not only reflects the emphasis on soundness of the evolving integrated market in financial services but also the global concerns that gave rise to the recommendations of the Cooke Committee.[72]

Additional harmonization steps are being taken or planned in such related areas as deposit guarantee schemes and other consumer protection measures in financial services; investment services in the securities field; and mortgage credit regulations. Overall, the directives and additional Commission recommendations will guide the member states toward a unified legal and regulatory setting for the internal market in capital and financial services. Given full capital liberalization, the single, competitive financial market will provide "borderless" access for residents to banking services, stock exchanges, real estate markets, and other financial services throughout the Community.

The prospect of free capital flows among members of the ERM and closer financial integration has given rise to concern about the sustainability of the EMS.[73] It has been argued that capital controls have been an essential element in securing the stability of the EMS, not only allowing some countries a limited degree of autonomy in their monetary policy, but also providing a safety valve against speculative capital movements. Without capital controls, there would be the risk of large speculative capital flows that would either require interest rate changes of a magnitude not acceptable to most countries, or would exert such pressure on exchange rates that the system would break up. But another view has held that the liberalization of capital movements would not necessarily trigger large-scale speculation as long as convergent and credible monetary policies were maintained in participating countries. In fact, liberalization would enhance credibility

---

[67] "The principle of subsidiarity" defines the functions of higher levels of government as subsidiary to those of lower levels. In the EC context, the principle implies that the ceding of authority by the lower levels to the Community level should be limited to that minimum of collective decision making which is indispensable for the functioning of agreed Community policies and mechanisms. Under the "principle of harmonization," Community rules, adopted to secure the necessary degree of coordination and commonality, enjoy pre-eminence over members' national rules. Under the "principle of mutual recognition," members agree to recognize each other's national rules where no Community rule has been established.

[68] Council Directive 88/361/EEC of June 24, 1988 for the Implementation of Article 67 of the Treaty, OJ, L 178, July 8, 1988.

[69] Second Council Directive 89/646/EEC of December 15, 1989 (OJ, L 386/1, December 30, 1989) on the coordination of laws, regulations, and administrative provisions relating to the taking up and pursuit of the business of credit institutions and amending Directive 77/780/EEC.

[70] Council Directive 89/647/EEC of December 18, 1988, OJ, L 386/14, December 30, 1989.

[71] Council Directive 89/299/EEC, OJ, L 124, May 5, 1989.

[72] The Committee on Banking Regulation and Supervisory Practices of the Bank for International Settlements (the Cooke Committee) was established in December 1975. In 1986, it proposed common definition, notably by the major industrial countries, of capital requirements for international banks, linked to banks' risk exposure. In 1987, the United Kingdom and the United States, joined later that year by Japan, proposed convergence of their systems for monitoring banks' capital adequacy. On this basis, the central bank governors of the Group of Ten countries in July 1988 endorsed a plan to harmonize minimum capital adequacy standards for international commercial banks. Apart from the coordinated approach now under way within the EC, the accord is implemented individually by the national authorities.

[73] For a review of the discussion on the consequences of full capital mobility for the EMS, see Mayer (1989) and Schröder (1989).

and exert a strong incentive to strive toward even greater convergence.[74]

Clearly, the risks mentioned and difficulties associated with the liberalization of capital movements should neither be ignored nor exaggerated. The staff of the EC Commission noted in a 1988 study that the envisaged extension of the ERM to all EC members, together with the joint commitment to the free movement of capital, would inevitably make the system "far more sensitive, from the point of view of the variability of interest and/or exchange rates, to cyclical lags and to the expectations of economic groups."[75] The mastering of the more complex system was seen to require a substantial reinforcement of convergence as well as increasingly effective coordination of the monetary policies of ERM participants. But if these preconditions were convincingly met, monetary stability in conjunction with free capital movements could boost confidence as the participating currencies would be fully exposed to market forces.

Experience of the recent past suggests that the fears of destabilizing effects of capital liberalization may have been unfounded. Contrary to widespread expectations, the removal of capital controls in several EC countries, in particular in France and Italy in January and May 1990, respectively, has not triggered capital *outflows* but has contributed to capital *inflows* by increasing the attractiveness of the respective currencies for international investors. To the extent that national authorities maintain policies that justify market confidence in their currencies, a sudden reversal of these flows appears unlikely. Thus, the full exposure of ERM currencies to market forces is apt to introduce greater policy discipline to the system and, therefore, to contribute to greater stability of the EMS—which, of course, is essential for the move toward economic and monetary union.

Liberalization of Capital Movements in the EC

The Capital Liberalization Directive of 1988

The directive adopted by the EC Council of Ministers in June 1988 stipulates for most EC countries the complete liberalization of capital movements by July 1, 1990. It builds on the extensive liberalization of capital movements and integration of financial markets that has been achieved in recent years. Beyond the earlier

formal liberalization steps within the EC, all short-term capital transactions (with a term of less than one year) were to be fully liberalized under the new directive, whether or not related to any underlying current account transactions or their financing. An important implication of this change is that member countries have undertaken to allow any short-term capital flows, monetary movements, shifts in leads and lags, speculative positions, etc., without restrictions.

The directive moves further toward equalizing the position of residents and nonresidents. The "ergo omnes" principle, extending the liberalization of most capital movements not only to other EC residents but to economic agents on a worldwide basis, is recommended as a general guideline for the implementation of the new directive. The principle shall not prejudice application of EC member countries' domestic rules or EC law to third countries, particularly as regards application of reciprocal conditions. Members will continue to be able, for instance, to exclude from liberalized treatment direct investments to particular non-EC countries. The liberalization of capital movements does not prevent EC countries from requiring residents to provide information about capital movements for statistical and fiscal purposes.

Should short-term capital movements of exceptional magnitude seriously disturb a member's foreign exchange market and the conduct of its monetary and exchange rate policies, it could resort to the EC's recently modified medium-term financial support facility (see Section II) or to specific safeguard clauses that allow the country to impose restrictions ("protective measures") on most categories of capital movements during a maximum period of six months. The country must inform the Commission and the partner countries, but their advance approval is not required. Where the disturbing capital movements relate to third (non-EC) countries, member countries shall consult each other about the measures to be taken, including a possible collective response by all EC countries.

The text of the directive records the requirement that by the end of December 1988 the EC Commission was to submit to the EC Council of Ministers proposals aimed at eliminating or reducing risks of distortion, tax evasion, and tax avoidance linked to the diversity of national systems for the taxation of savings and for controlling the application of these systems. Such proposals were duly submitted. The problem of tax evasion and the issue of the harmonization of taxes on capital transactions, such as a withholding tax on interest income, was particularly important and sensitive to those countries that rely relatively heavily on such taxes. The negotiations that ensued were prolonged and difficult. The compromises reached provide, inter alia, for a degree of cooperation between the authorities

---

[74] See, for example, Driffill (1988) and McDonald and others (1989).

[75] Commission of the European Communities (1988), p. 20.

of EC countries in combating tax evasion, but the pursuit of uniform or converging taxation of capital incomes was abandoned for the time being.

Progress of Capital Liberalization in EC Countries

Within the EC in the late 1960s, extensive liberalization of capital movements (far beyond the requirements of the EC directives of 1960 and 1963) had been achieved by Germany, Belgium-Luxembourg (although the latter maintained a dual foreign exchange market until early 1990), and, in most respects, the Netherlands. In the unsettled period in the capital markets that accompanied the twilight of the par value system around 1970, controls on capital movements were widely tightened. Even Germany in 1971 reintroduced capital restrictions, albeit only on inflows; these controls were lifted in stages in 1974, 1975, and 1981.

The United Kingdom held on to some of its particular capital controls more or less from the beginning of the First World War through the 1970s. Certain restrictions were abolished ahead of the accession of the United Kingdom to the EC in 1973, and further progress was achieved in 1977. Important controls on direct and portfolio investment, residents' foreign currency deposits, and sterling lending to nonresidents were lifted in 1979, with complete liberalization of capital movements in effect from October 24, 1979.

In Italy, the progress toward the abolition of the remaining few but significant capital controls was until recently blocked by concerns about potentially destabilizing capital flows and about the costs and patterns of servicing the heavy debt of the public sector. In September 1987, when the lira was subject to exchange market pressure, controls on short-term trade-related capital movements were intensified. However, the authorities basically supported EC-wide efforts toward the complete capital liberalization that was implicit in the Single European Act. With the entry into force of new legislation in October 1988, the overall regulatory attitude was decisively shifted in favor of liberalization of capital movements. Thereafter, capital transactions vis-à-vis nonresidents were permitted unless they were specifically restricted. A surrender requirement in respect of foreign exchange receipts was generally maintained, short-term investments remained controlled, and residents were not allowed to maintain deposits abroad. In January 1990, in conjunction with a devaluation of the lira within the ERM and acceptance by Italy of the narrow margins of the ERM for the lira (see Section III), short-term capital movements were freed and the surrender requirement abolished.

Residents' deposits abroad were liberalized as from May 14, 1990, completing the liberalization of all capital movements.

France, like Italy, had during 1968–73 reintensified capital controls. In the 1980s, even as the EMS was gaining strength and credibility, the French view seems to have remained reserved: "Overall, the EMS is seen as a most useful arrangement which should not be endangered by unwarranted expectations about the benefits of financial integration."[76] A program of gradual liberalization of exchange and capital controls was nevertheless adopted in 1983 that resulted in important steps, particularly in 1986 and at the beginning of 1989. Effective January 1, 1990, the remaining restriction prohibiting French residents from holding in France deposits denominated in a foreign currency (other than the ECU) and from holding deposits abroad, was abolished; at the same time, all remaining restrictions on lending to nonresidents were lifted.

Denmark abolished all remaining exchange restrictions and controls on capital movements, effective October 1, 1988. The right of residents to hold deposits abroad does not apply to residents of Greenland, which is no longer a part of the EC, and the liberalization has not yet become effective in the Faeroe Islands.

The capital liberalization directive of June 1988 was to be in general incorporated in members' national legislation by end-June 1990. However, in view of member countries' varied development level and balance of payments strength, the directive recognizes the specific derogations (expiring in 1990–92), which allow Spain and Portugal under their Act of Accession to maintain certain capital controls previously abolished by the EC. In addition, Greece, Ireland, Portugal, and Spain are allowed until end-1992 to maintain or reintroduce restrictions on most categories of capital movements; an extension of up to three years (through 1995) may be approved for Greece and Portugal. Moving in some respects ahead of the special schedules allowed, the four less industrialized EC countries have recently introduced additional though limited liberalization measures and have intensified their efforts to achieve full capital liberalization in the period ahead. As in the past with other EC countries, the liberalization of the often unpredictable short-term capital movements not related to underlying current account transactions is approached cautiously and gradually. For Ireland, the background for the slower transition to full liberalization included (until October 1990) the nonparticipation of the United Kingdom, Ireland's key commercial and financial partner, in the ERM.

[76] Wyplosz (1988b), p. 87.

The Second Banking Directive

On December 15, 1989, the Council of Ministers adopted the Second Banking Directive. Its purpose is to govern the authorization of credit institutions and the provision of financial services throughout the EC. In the pursuit of this purpose, it relies fundamentally on the implementation of the principles of mutual recognition of members' rules for the licensing and regulation of banks, extensive home country control of credit institutions throughout the Community, and joint prudential norms for credit institutions. The member countries of the EC are to adapt their laws and regulations to reach compliance with the new directive by January 1, 1993.

Under the new directive, an EC-based credit institution authorized in its "home" member country (the EC country that has issued the institution's banking license) to conduct any or all banking activities subject to mutual recognition is allowed to conduct the same kinds of business throughout the EC. The list of banking activities subject to mutual recognition is quite comprehensive. The "single banking license" is thereby given a very broad definition, while home country regulations apply in principle in most respects and especially in authorization and prudential matters. The combination may result in cases in which authority must be granted to a "guest" bank to conduct listed activities even when some of these are not allowed by the host country for its "own" authorized banks. This is intended to create pressure toward broadening the permitted activities of the latter banks, resulting in a tendency toward uniformly broad banking authorization.

The "host" country will retain complete responsibility for monetary policy in respect of all credit institutions operating in its territory, without discrimination based on the fact that a credit institution is authorized in another member state. With respect to surveillance of the market risk assumed by each bank, close cooperation between home country and host country authorities is envisaged. In addition to the monetary policy aspect mentioned, many host country rules governing the conduct of financial institutions will still apply, in principle, regardless of the country of authorization of the banks.

Having met the harmonized authorization conditions, such as the minimum initial capital generally of ECU 5 million, an authorized credit institution may operate branches in any member country without further authorization or endowment capital requirements. The authorization in a member country of a subsidiary of a bank authorized in another member country is subject to prior consultation between the two governments. This control is of a prudential nature; basically

subsidiaries enjoy the same freedoms of establishment and activity as independent banks. An authorized credit institution may also provide services throughout the Community in a cross-border fashion, without establishment.

Noting that the liberalization of capital movements and the liberalization of the provision of financial services in the EC need to proceed in harmony, the new directive recognizes the right of a member country to suspend temporarily the implementation of the liberalized banking services if disturbances resulting from short-term capital movements force it to impose temporary restrictions on some categories of capital movements, availing itself of the above-mentioned safeguard clauses of the capital liberalization directive of 1988.

The international setting for the Second Banking Directive is characterized by increasingly interdependent financial markets. At the same time as major banks based in EC countries operate in third markets, large transnational banks from all parts of the world have been established in EC countries. The directive underlines that "the Community intends to keep its financial markets open to the rest of the world." Since the new banking licenses of credit institutions, including those based in third countries, will have EC-wide rather than national application, they will improve the access also of third-country banks to the EC-wide financial area. Within the EC, this has given rise to demands for a reciprocity in the authorization from the third countries. As existing bilateral reciprocity in banking authorization practices of individual members is replaced by Community-wide reciprocity, the directive envisages that reciprocity will be operated by the EC to promote parallel liberalization in financial markets of non-EC countries, thus seeking increased competitive opportunities for EC-based banks in such markets.

Under the new directive, the authorities of each EC member country undertake to notify the EC Commission whenever a banking authorization is granted to the subsidiary of an institution based outside the EC area and when a bank authorized in a member country becomes the subsidiary of such an outside institution. The Commission will monitor the treatment accorded to EC-based banks in third countries. The directive provides for negotiations with a third country when needed to pursue for EC-based banks effective market access comparable to that granted by the EC to credit institutions from that third country. In view of the nondiscriminatory treatment accorded in the new EC-wide financial market to banks regardless of their origin, a more rigorous insistence on the reciprocity of rights of establishment and operation is prescribed for the pursuit in third countries of the "minimum" aim of "national treatment" for EC-based financial institutions.[77] Where such national treatment ("treatment offering the same competitive opportunities as are available to domestic credit institutions" of the third country in question) is perceived as being denied, the Commission may proceed to negotiations to rectify the situation. In the meantime, the EC may also decide that member countries must limit or suspend the processing of requests from the third country for new banking licenses, bank participations, and acquisitions within the EC.

The subsidiaries of parent banks based outside the EC, once approved by one EC country, are eligible to obtain the new single, EC-wide banking license, with the same freedom of establishment and operation as those enjoyed by banks based in EC countries and their subsidiaries. Institutions thus authorized are not subject to possible subsequent reciprocity-related EC sanctions as described above. Branches in EC countries of third-country banks (when not managed by a subsidiary in an EC member country) do not gain the new single banking license or the extensive freedom of establishment and operation associated with it. Rather, such branches (unlike subsidiaries) remain subject to existing laws and bilateral understandings.

---

[77] The background of the national treatment approach is discussed in Folkerts-Landau and Mathieson (1989), p. 19.

The Solvency Directive

Within the set of new financial sector directives and recommendations, the Solvency Directive represents the indispensable main prudential complement to the more broadly policy-shaping Second Banking Directive. The basic aim of the Solvency Directive is to establish an appropriate, sufficiently high solvency ratio with the aim of harmonizing and strengthening the solvency of financial institutions and its prudential supervision across the EC. The applicable solvency ratio is designed to weight specific assets and off-balance-sheet items according to the degree of risk involved. At the same time, the directive emphasizes undistorted competition among credit institutions in the common banking market. Therefore, the solvency standards are to be uniformly applied, so that the minimum solvency ratio from January 1, 1991 will stand at 8 percent, with very limited exceptions.

The solvency ratio, as defined in the directive, expresses the own funds of a credit institution (the specifications and prudential norms for own funds having been set in the Own Funds Directive) as a proportion of its risk-adjusted total assets, including off-balance-sheet items. The degree of credit risk is expressed as a percentage weight, specific to each type of asset. The book value of each asset is multiplied by its prescribed percentage weight to obtain its risk-adjusted value for the denominator of the solvency ratio.

V Monetary Integration in the European Community

The Internal Market Program and Monetary Integration

Two developments in the EC in the monetary and financial area stand out in the last several years: the achievements and the consolidation of the EMS, and the adoption of the internal market program.

The first development—the success of the EMS—has led to the question of how the stability of the EMS can be enhanced and a more efficient framework provided for future cooperation in exchange rate and monetary policies. Those who favor the institutional development of the system have stressed the desire to rely less on discretion and more on rules and to shift emphasis from reliance on the policies of the dominant country to common policies. Others, however, have questioned whether substantial institutional changes are needed and whether it would not be sufficient, and more desirable, to rely on more efficient policy coordination within the existing framework. In this way, past achievements would not be put in jeopardy.

The other development—the implementation of the internal market program—goes beyond the scope of financial integration. It promises the realization of still unattained objectives set by the founding fathers of the European Communities in the 1950s, in particular the establishment of a truly common market as the basis for the full economic integration of the EC countries, for closer political cooperation and greater social cohesion, and for higher standards of living of all citizens of the EC.

It has been argued that the implementation of the internal market program would have to be supported by a common monetary policy and monetary union. The optimal results of the internal market could only be achieved if the monetary arrangements for the EC were to minimize, if not eliminate, the uncertainties resulting from independent national monetary policies and from exchange rates subject to adjustments and fluctuations. The argument can be summed up under the dictum of the "inconsistent quartet," that is, the incompatibility of free trade, full capital mobility, fixed exchange rates, and national autonomy in the conduct of monetary policy.[78]

On the other hand, it has been pointed out that at present monetary policies are not conducted in full independence nor are exchange rates completely fixed. The EMS Agreement provided for fluctuation margins offering some flexibility and for the possibility of central rate changes, which could compensate for diverging monetary policies. As divergences narrowed, central rate adjustments could be (and, on the last two occasions in January 1987 and January 1990, were) small so as not to affect market rates, thus minimizing the potential for destabilizing capital flows. What was important for realizing the internal market—it was argued—was not so much to aim at fixed *nominal* exchange rates as to achieve a high degree of stability in *real* exchange rates. Most important, this goal required a consolidation of economic convergence and policy credibility, as achieved among a number of core countries in the ERM, and their extension to other EC members.

It is generally agreed, however, that the realization of the internal market and progress toward economic and monetary union demand a high degree of policy consistency and compatibility (whether by coordination or by common policies based on and secured by institutional arrangements) if serious disruptions of the internal market and the emergence of pronounced regional and structural imbalances are to be averted.

Strategies of Monetary Integration

In essence there are three paths to closer monetary integration: the parallel-currency approach; a high degree of policy coordination; and commonly defined and decided policies, with the ultimate objective of

---

[78] See Padoa-Schioppa (1988), p. 373. See also Folkerts-Landau and Mathieson (1989), p. 1.

common institutions, a common policy, and a common single currency.[79]

The parallel-currency approach has a long history: there are a number of cases where more than one currency circulated simultaneously in one country, whether by common practice or by institutional design. In the context of European economic integration, this approach was particularly advocated in the 1970s.[80] The most common approach in the EC context has been to suggest the introduction of a European monetary unit that would circulate alongside existing national currencies and that by institutional design would be more stable than the national currencies, for example, by pegging its value to an index of goods. Such a European parallel currency could successfully compete with national currencies and gradually replace them. Ideas to use an existing national currency on an EC-wide scale have been largely rejected because of political implications. The present ECU has been found wanting because of its basket composition; it would always be weaker than several of its composite currencies and therefore could not effectively compete with them.

However, the concept of an institutionally strong parallel currency has also run into strong objections. As such a currency gained in importance, it would have to be managed in coordination with national currencies. Instead of having to coordinate the management of X currencies, X plus 1 currencies would have to be coordinated. This was considered a cumbersome detour to a common monetary policy, requiring at the beginning of the process the common arrangements it was supposed to pave the way for.[81] Furthermore, "an additional source of money creation without a precise linkage to economic activity could jeopardize price stability."[82]

Those who advocate a more intensified effort to coordinate policies before common institutional arrangements are contemplated point to the still existing divergences in economic performance as well as to differences in economic structure and social and political attitudes to economic problems in various countries. Instead of advocating additional institutional constraints, they emphasize the disciplinary aspects of existing arrangements, in particular the ERM, and the more flexible approach of narrowing existing differences through closer cooperation that would also respect national sensitivities and sovereignty. This approach is often referred to as a "hardening of the EMS."[83] But such an approach is time consuming and such cooperation is basically voluntary. Owing to its decentralized decision-making process, it is less suited to coping with sudden emergencies and to ensuring progress toward common policy positions that would keep pace with the rapidly advancing economic and financial integration in the EC. It would also tend to perpetuate the asymmetric aspects of the EMS.

A determined move toward common policymaking and economic and monetary union has been supported mainly by France, Italy, and Spain, and also by the EC Commission.[84] The basic argument described above was that the internal market needed a strong and clearly defined institutional framework for common policies suitable to meet both its economic challenges once completed and the political requirements of a community of nations in dealing with its own further development as well as the increasingly closer interdependence of the world economy.

The debate on the best way of fostering monetary cooperation and integration of the EC brought up again a basic difference in approach that had dominated the debates on monetary integration in the 1960s. It has often been cast in terms of a debate between the "monetarists" and "economists"—those who favor strong reliance on the building of institutional monetary arrangements, and those who favor a gradual approach, with strong emphasis on narrowing existing differences in economic policies and developments and, in the longer run, also in basic economic and social conditions. The first group argued that common objectives in the field of monetary policy can best and most rapidly be achieved by introducing institutional commitments and constraints. The second held that a consensus has to be reached about economic policy priorities and a very high convergence of economic performance achieved before moving to common institutional arrangements in the monetary field.

---

[79] Russo and Tullio (1988, pp. 57–62) discuss in some detail four possible models of commonly agreed monetary policies that would go beyond discretionary coordination. While these rules do not imply a common policy based on a common monetary institution, they represent alternate approaches that could be followed by a common institution, such as a European central bank.

[80] See Basevi and others (1975), Commission of the European Communities (1975) and (1976), and Vaubel (1978). More recently, see Russo (1988). See also the most recent proposal of the U.K. authorities, pages 43–44, below.

[81] See Szász (1988) and Duisenberg (1989a).

[82] Committee for the Study of Economic and Monetary Union, *Report on Economic and Monetary Union in the European Community* (Luxembourg, 1989) (henceforth Delors Report), p. 33. For a general critical review of the parallel-currency approach, see Kloten and Bofinger (1988).

[83] It has been favored by the Board of Academic Advisers to the German Federal Ministry of Economics (Wissenschaftlicher Beirat beim Bundesministerium für Wirtschaft, 1989a). Similar ideas can be found in the proposals of the U.K. Treasury, see below. See also Currie (1989).

[84] Also advocated by the Committee for the Monetary Union of Europe (1988) and the Committee on Economic and Monetary Affairs and Industrial Policy of the European Parliament (1989).

Debate About Future Monetary Integration in the EC

The debate about the experiences with the EMS and the future direction of monetary cooperation and integration started out in the mid-1980s with discussions on more technical issues. These issues—intervention practices, conditions of access to the very short-term financing facility of the EMS, the role of the ECU—are nevertheless important for monetary policy and its general objectives. Initially, the debate was conducted between senior officials of governments, central banks, and the EC Commission in forums such as the Committee of Central Bank Governors and its working groups, and the Monetary Committee.[85] Parallel to discussions on the official level, and at times intertwined with them, academic debates have been taking place in economic journals and at conferences and symposia organized by universities and similarly independent research and policy-oriented institutions.[86]

The debate about the form and objectives of monetary cooperation and integration gained significant momentum and an additional, political dimension in the early months of 1988. Politicians from various EC countries addressed the issue of economic and monetary union in the EC and expressed their support, though with a different degree of urgency.[87] Also, academics, nonofficial groups, and senior central bank officials, speaking in a personal capacity, put forward detailed proposals of how and under what conditions a common European monetary authority and a common currency could be established.[88]

The subject of economic and monetary union became a prominent item on the agenda of the regular half-yearly meetings of the heads of state and governments of the EC countries, the European Council. At its meeting in Hanover on June 27 and 28, 1988, the Council set up a special committee charged with "studying and proposing concrete stages leading towards [economic and monetary] union." The Committee, named after its chairman, EC Commission President Jacques Delors,

was composed of the central bank governors of the 12 EC countries, an additional member of the EC Commission, and 3 outside experts. The Committee presented its report in April 1989, which was subsequently discussed by the Monetary Committee and by the economics and finance ministers of the EC countries at their meeting in Antibes in April 1989. Meeting in Madrid on June 26 and 27, 1989, the European Council asked the Council of Ministers, the Committee of Central Bank Governors, and the Monetary Committee "to adopt the provisions necessary for the launch of the first stage [as proposed in the report of the Delors Committee] on July 1, 1990 [and] to carry out the preparatory work for the organization of an intergovernmental conference to lay down the subsequent stages." On December 8–9, 1989, the European Council agreed in Strasbourg to convene an intergovernmental conference before the end of 1990, "charged with preparing an amendment of the EEC Treaty with a view to the final stages of economic and monetary union."

The Delors Report

Summary of the Delors Report

The Delors Committee proposed in its report[89] the realization of economic and monetary union in three stages, with parallel progression in the economic and monetary field. Instead of deadlines for the transition from one stage to another, it proposed that the beginning of each stage should be decided depending on the progress achieved during the preceding stage.

In the report, monetary union was defined as the total and irreversible convertibility of currencies; the complete liberalization of capital movements and the full integration of financial markets; the elimination of fluctuation margins and the irreversible locking of exchange rates. Economic union was defined as a single market within which persons, goods, services, and capital can freely move; a joint competition policy to strengthen market mechanisms; common structural and regional policies; and macroeconomic policy coordination including binding rules for budgetary policies regarding the size and financing of national budget deficits. "Economic union and monetary union form *two integral parts of a single whole* and would therefore have to be implemented in parallel" (p.18).

---

[85] Since these discussions are usually confidential, no published records exist. However, speeches and interviews by such officials shed some light on the nature of the issues discussed.

[86] *Economic and Social Review*—"European Monetary System: 10th Anniversary Issue," ed. by Michael Moore, Vol. 20 (January 1989); *Journal of Common Market Studies*—Special Issue: The European Monetary System (March 1989); De Grauwe and Peeters (1989); Giavazzi, Micossi, and Miller (1988); de Cecco and Giovannini (1989); Conference at the University of Bergamo, "The European Monetary System, Ten Years Later" (May 1989; unpublished); and Welfens (1990).

[87] Amato (1988), Balladur (1988), Genscher (1988), and Stoltenberg (1988).

[88] Committee for the Monetary Union of Europe (1988), Gros and Thygesen (1988), Kloten (1988), Dini (1988), and Duisenberg (1988).

---

[89] All page references in this paper are to the edition of the report cited in fn. 82 above. In a second part, the publication contains a collection of papers submitted to the Committee by individual committee members. These papers either deal with specific aspects of EMU or represent preparatory position papers.

At the heart of the Delors Report was the proposal to set up a European System of Central Banks (ESCB) as the way to creating a monetary union and a common single currency. While a single currency was not considered strictly necessary for the creation of a monetary union, it was seen—for economic as well as psychological and political reasons—as a natural and desirable further development of the monetary union.

The report underlined that an essential element for an appropriate balance of powers within the EC would be adherence to the "principle of subsidiarity." Under this principle, "the functions of higher levels of government should be as limited as possible and should be subsidiary to those of lower levels" (p.18).

The ESCB should be organized in a federal form and consist of a central institution and the national central banks. An ESCB Council would be composed of the governors of the central banks and the members of the board, the latter to be appointed by the European Council. The ESCB would be committed to the objective of price stability. Subject to the foregoing, the ESCB should support the general economic policy set at the Community level by the competent bodies. The ESCB would be responsible for formulating and implementing monetary policy, exchange rate and reserve management, and for maintaining a properly functioning payments system. It would not lend to public sector authorities. For the fulfillment of its tasks, it would be provided with the necessary instruments. The ESCB Council should be independent of instructions from national governments and Community authorities. The national central banks would be entrusted with implementing the common monetary policy, in conformity with the guidelines established by the ESCB Council.

In the field of economic policy, the report did not propose the creation of a new institution. Rather, the roles of existing bodies, such as the Council of Ministers and the Commission, would be modified and extended, and the areas would be determined in which decision-making authority would have to be transferred from the national to the Community level.

Stage one would aim at a greater convergence of economic performance through the strengthening of economic and monetary policy coordination within the existing institutional framework. In the economic field, stage one would center on the completion of the internal market and the reduction of existing regional disparities. In the monetary field, the objective of a single financial area would be fully implemented. All EC currencies should participate in the EMS exchange rate mechanism, and all impediments to the private use of the ECU would be removed. The mandate of the Committee of Central Bank Governors would be expanded. The Committee would formulate opinions on the overall orientation of monetary and exchange rate policy and would forward opinions to individual governments and to the Council of Ministers on policies affecting the monetary situation in the Community, especially the functioning of the EMS. It would submit annual reports on its activities and on the monetary situation in the EC to the European Parliament and the European Council. The Committee would set up three subcommittees for monetary policy analysis, foreign exchange policy, and banking supervision, and provide them with a permanent research staff.

Stage two would be a period of transition and constitute a learning process leading to collective decision making. In the monetary field, the most important feature would be the setting up of the ESCB, which would absorb previously existing institutions such as the European Monetary Cooperation Fund, the Committee of Central Bank Governors and its subcommittees, and the permanent secretariat. The key task for the ESCB would be to begin the transition from the coordination of independent monetary policies to the formulation and implementation of a common monetary policy. The margins of fluctuation within the ERM would be narrowed, subject to progress in convergence. A certain amount of exchange reserves would be pooled and used to conduct exchange market interventions, in accordance with ESCB guidelines.

The final stage would start with a move to irrevocably locked exchange rates. In the economic field, common structural and regional policies would be further strengthened, and rules in the macroeconomic and budgetary field would become binding. The transition to a single monetary policy would be made, and the ESCB would assume all its responsibilities. Decisions on exchange market interventions in third currencies would become the sole responsibility of the ESCB Council, and official reserves would be pooled and managed by the ESCB. The changeover to a single currency would take place during this stage.

Since the EEC Treaty, as amended by the Single European Act, was insufficient for the full realization of economic and monetary union, a new treaty would be required. The report listed two options: a new treaty for each stage, and a single comprehensive treaty for the process as a whole. The Committee expressed a preference for the latter approach and called for a clear political commitment to the final stage, that is, to the full realization of economic and monetary union.

Viewed against the debates of the past twenty or thirty years or so in the EC about the underlying principal as well as the more practical aspects of monetary cooperation, the report of the Delors Committee represents an effort to come to a common position on a number of aspects. It adopts neither a strongly "monetarist" nor "economist" view as discussed above, but advocates parallel progress in establishing monetary and economic union, thus accepting a broadly held consensus that the building of institutions and the strengthening of policy coordination influence each other in a mutual and dynamic fashion. This approach can also be seen as an amalgamation of the strategies, characterized above, of striving toward institutionalization and of ''hardening the EMS,'' in particular in stage one but to a certain degree also in stage two.

The Delors Report and the Werner Report

Nearly two decades separate the preparation of the Delors Report from the first comprehensive attempt of the EC to define and move toward EMU, exemplified by the Werner Report. During this period, the EC grew from the original 6 founding members to a membership of 12 countries. The worldwide economic environment underwent substantial changes ranging from the collapse of the Bretton Woods system to shifts in the relative economic importance of major countries. Against this background, it may be interesting to compare the main features of the report of the Delors Committee with those of the report of the Werner Committee. The Werner Committee was set up in 1970 on the initiative of the heads of state and government of the six EC countries at a conference in The Hague in December 1969, and was chaired by Pierre Werner, then Prime Minister of Luxembourg. The two committees share a similar genesis: both were established on initiatives at the highest level of government of the EC countries, reflecting the concern over further progress in integration and recognizing the importance of closer monetary cooperation for economic integration. Both committees favored the parallel advancement of economic and monetary union and suggested a common single European currency as the ultimate goal. In defining EMU, the Delors Committee relied explicitly on the work of the Werner Committee.

But the two committees deliberated, and the reports were written, against different political and economic backgrounds. In 1969, the EC still consisted of the original six members, which—with the partial exception of Italy—had similar economic structures. In 1968, the customs union, as planned in the EEC Treaty, had been completed, and a common trade policy had been adopted, and earlier a common market for most agricultural goods had been established. In the exchange rate field, in the 1960s, the prevailing philosophy, in line with the principles of the IMF Articles of Agreement, was that stable if not fixed exchange rates were highly desirable as well as feasible. The international monetary crises of 1967, leading to the devaluation of sterling, and of 1968 and 1969, culminating in the temporary floating and eventually a significant revaluation of the

deutsche mark and a similarly sizable devaluation of the French franc, were seen as a threat to the stability of the EEC and its further development. In the event, in part owing to the breakdown of the Bretton Woods system and the transition to worldwide floating in 1973, the EMU as proposed in the Werner Report never got off the ground. The main outgrowth of these efforts was the establishment of the European common margins arrangement (the snake) in April 1972. In reality, the snake did not so much serve as a stepping stone to EMU—as envisaged in the Werner Report—but rather provided a degree of monetary cohesion and exchange rate stability for a limited number of EC countries in an environment of worldwide floating. While the snake started with all EC countries (including the new members of 1973, the United Kingdom, Ireland, and Denmark) as well as Norway and Sweden participating, it gradually shrank to a few currencies (including those of Norway and Sweden) being grouped around the deutsche mark. The other larger EC countries (France, Italy, and the United Kingdom) had left the arrangement.

The Delors Report can be seen against the background of an international exchange rate system where floating currencies coexisted with currencies that were pegged to another currency or a basket of currencies. The Delors Committee could also draw on the experiences that EC countries, and in particular their central banks, had with the management of the snake and, since 1979, with the policies and operations in the framework of the EMS. The Committee had to take account also of the greater diversity of EC membership, which with the accession of Greece, Portugal, and Spain numbered 12, and of the fact that several of the EC members (namely, Greece, Portugal, Spain—until June 1989—and the United Kingdom–until October 1990) were not participating in the ERM.

Both reports proposed the creation of the EMU in three stages. The Werner Report suggested completing a first stage in two years and the whole process of establishing the EMU in ten years. The Delors Report did not set any deadlines for either the process as a whole or its individual stages. Both reports envisaged the creation of a common European central bank. While the Werner Report recommended also a decision center for economic policy, the Delors Report saw no need for this. The Delors Report advocated a federalized European central bank that would be independent of instructions from European or national institutions, with price stability as its main objective, clearly modeled on the institutional arrangements in Germany. The Werner Report did not pronounce itself as clearly on the institutional setup of a European central bank system and did not identify the main objective for a common monetary policy.[90] With regard to coordination of fiscal policy, however, the Werner Report went further than the Delors Report by not only urging binding rules for budgetary policies on the size and financing of budget deficits but also recommending a more general harmonization of budget policies, comprising their main elements (notably total receipts and expenditures) and the distribution of the latter between investment and consumption. In general, whereas the Werner Report was more process and procedure oriented in its concrete proposals, the Delors Report devoted more attention to policy objectives and the institutional framework of common economic and monetary policies.[91]

Discussion of the Delors Report

Not surprisingly, the Delors Report and its proposals were received quite differently depending on the views prevailing on the speed and form that closer monetary cooperation should take. On the one hand, there were those (exemplified by France and Italy) who—based on what they perceived to be the great challenges of European integration—argued for speedy moves toward common institutions and policies; on the other, there were those (represented mainly by Germany and the Netherlands) who felt that an extended period of closer cooperation and more economic convergence (more or less circumscribed by the proposed first stage of the Delors Report) was required before more far-reaching institutional arrangements could be put in place. In the United Kingdom, public opinion in journals and newspapers partly supported the proposals while official reaction was tentative. At the highest level of government it was clearly negative: the Delors Report represented only one way to closer monetary integration, and not a preferred one. While the U.K. authorities favored pressing ahead with the internal market program, including the integration of the financial sector, they did not consider a commitment to EMU at this stage either necessary or desirable.[92]

The following sections summarize the main points in the debate on some important issues raised by the Delors Report, but no attempt is made to resolve them.

The U.K. Proposals for EMU

Following the meeting of the European Council in Madrid in June 1989, the U.K. authorities presented their concept of how to proceed with monetary cooperation in the EC.[93] Instead of the "institutional" approach of the Delors Report, centering on the establishment of a European System of Central Banks and the ultimate creation of a common single currency, the paper offered an "evolutionary approach." This approach would allow existing national currencies to compete with each other in a multicurrency system to ensure stable prices and thus stable exchange rates. It would be centered on national monetary authorities and would therefore minimize problems of political accountability. The EMS could evolve into a system of more or less fixed exchange rates, and a "practical monetary union" would be achieved.

The argument can be summarized as follows. Stage one, as proposed in the Delors Report, would reshape the EC economies. The liberalization of capital movements, rising currency substitution, and the increased mobility of labor would exert powerful stimuli for monetary authorities to pursue noninflationary policies to attract economic activity. The resulting move toward exchange rate stability would reduce uncertainty and lower the costs of the envisaged multicurrency system. Considerable evidence existed that these mechanisms already worked in practice, and that in recent years there had been greater convergence of inflation within the EMS and fewer realignments. During stage one, if its objectives were realized, inflationary pressures would be sharply reduced, and with them the pressure for exchange rate changes. After stage one, priority should be given to those measures that would assist and accelerate the beneficial trends toward economic and financial integration such as the removal of restrictions on the use of EC currencies. Greater use of the private ECU could also reduce transaction costs. ". . . these measures would strengthen the process of convergence on price and exchange rate stability. Realignments would become rarer, fluctuations within the ERM bands would become smaller, and the EMS could evolve into a system of more or less fixed exchange rates . . . . In this way a practical monetary union would be achieved as the result of a gradual evolutionary process."[94]

The U.K. proposals were met with widespread interest but also with pronounced criticism.[95] There was

---

[90] Of the seven members of the Werner Committee only two were central bankers.

[91] See also Gunter D. Baer and Tommaso Padoa-Schioppa, "The Werner Report Revisited," Delors Report, pp. 53-60.

[92] See the opinions expressed by the Chancellor of the Exchequer, Nigel Lawson, and the Prime Minister, Margaret Thatcher, respectively, before the Treasury and Civil Service Committee of the House of Commons, June 12, 1989, and before the House of Commons, June 29, 1989, United Kingdom (1989a).

[93] United Kingdom (1989b).

[94] United Kingdom (1989b), p. 5.

[95] For critical responses, see, for example, Ciampi (1989b), Costa (1989), and Carli (1990). For a supportive view, see Brittan (1989). A concept, which in many respects is similar to the U.K. proposals, was presented by the Board of Academic Advisers to the German Federal Ministry of Economics (Wissenschaftlicher Beirat beim Bundesministerium für Wirtschaft, 1989a).

general agreement regarding the emphasis on the completion of the internal market and in particular on further liberalization in the financial field. But there were also serious doubts whether a "competition of currencies" would result in a stable and desirable monetary order for the EC. As long as national currencies were not irrevocably linked to each other, one could not speak of a monetary union, even if policies were highly coordinated, nor could one expect the full benefits of a monetary union for a single market in terms of reducing transaction costs and eliminating exchange rate risks. Greater competition between currencies would actually increase rather than diminish the frequency and seriousness of bouts of instability. "The merest suspicion . . . that a country was diverging from the common monetary policy [directed toward stability] would shake the market's confidence," and exert pressure on exchange rates, and massive central bank intervention would follow (Ciampi). The stability of a monetary system "is achieved through the enactment of well defined, transparent, and consistent policies"; it was not competition among central banks but the coordination of policies that would bring about an orderly convergence. "The accumulated experience of many countries . . . does not suggest that [the use of parallel currencies and currency substitution] has forced monetary authorities to adopt low-inflation stances but rather that it has brought about unprecedented swings in money demand . . . ." (Carli). From a systemic point of view, it was argued that the competition of currencies, very much like the present asymmetric approach of the EMS (under which the system is anchored to one national currency, the deutsche mark), would eventually "result in the crowning of a national currency and its underlying economy to become the standards of the EC system." In comparison, the proposals of the Delors Report were "far more balanced and symmetrical" and therefore "more acceptable and realistic" (Costa). The EC Commission summed it up in this way: "Any attempt to base economic and monetary union on competition between monetary policies would lead either to one of the national monetary policies playing a dominant role or to the maintenance of different policies, which would then rule out irrevocably fixed exchange rates."[96]

In June 1990, the U.K. Chancellor of the Exchequer, John Major, presented a new proposal which supplemented that of November 1989. It stressed the need to strive for more convergence in economic performance: "Without greatly increased convergence, monetary union simply would not work."[97] The proposal envisaged an important role for the ECU in monetary inte-

gration, by having it exist alongside and compete with national currencies. As a first step, a European Monetary Fund (EMF) would be created that would issue ECUs on demand against EC currencies. A second step would be the creation of a "hard ECU" as a genuine currency, which would never devalue against other EC currencies.[98] The EMF would then issue deposits and notes denominated in hard ECUs in exchange for national currencies. There would be an obligation for all EC central banks to repurchase their own currencies from the EMF for hard currencies. Since no new money would be created, there would be no inflationary threat. In addition, the EMF could take on additional functions such as managing the ERM and its financing facilities, medium-term balance of payments lending, and coordinating EC countries' intervention against third currencies. In time, the ECU would be more widely used; it could become a common currency and, in the very long run, the single currency for the EC.

The new U.K. proposals left a number of questions open, such as the institutional features of the EMF, and met with quite some skepticism.[99] Some considered the repurchase obligation a powerful sanction against lax monetary policies, similar to the threat of a gold drain under the Gold Standard, or a reserve drain under the Bretton Woods system. The main perceived shortcoming of the proposal was, however, "that it provides little guidance on when the conditions are right for moving to the final stage of full monetary union."[100]

Coordination of Fiscal Policies

The Delors Report was very careful in pointing out at various places that economic and monetary union had to be implemented in parallel and stressed that "the integration process . . . requires *more intensive and effective policy coordination* . . . . While *voluntary co-operation* should be relied upon as much as possible . . . there is also likely to be a need for more binding procedures" (p.15). The report also mentioned, as one of the shortcomings of the EMS, "the lack of sufficient convergence of fiscal policies," (p.12). It was argued that "unco-ordinated and divergent national budgetary policies would undermine monetary stability and generate imbalances in the real and financial sectors of the Community"; since the Community budget could not play any significant role, mainly because of its size, "the task of setting a Community-wide fiscal policy

---

[96] Commission of the European Communities (1990a).
[97] Major (1990), para. 12.

[98] This concept of a "hard ECU" was not entirely new; similar proposals had been presented before. See Commission of the European Communities (1975) and Russo (1988).
[99] See, for example, Pöhl (1990b).
[100] Brittan (1990).

stance will have to be performed through the coordination of national budgetary policies . . . . Monetary policy alone cannot be expected to perform these functions'' (pp. 23 and 24). It therefore argued for binding rules that would "impose effective upper limits on budget deficits of individual member countries . . . , exclude access to direct central bank credit and other forms of monetary financing, . . . [and] limit recourse to external borrowing in non-Community currencies'' (p.24). Rules for budgetary policy would have to include "the definition of the overall stance of fiscal policy over the medium term, including the size and financing of the aggregate budgetary balance, comprising both the national and the Community positions'' (p.28).

Such views have triggered a wide-ranging debate. It is generally agreed that monetary and budgetary policies need to be compatible and that no or only limited recourse to monetary financing should be available. Also, undisciplined governments should not be bailed out. In question is whether the compatibility of policies can best be achieved by market forces, intensified coordination between individual countries, or centralization at the Community level.

It has been argued that without central bank financing and with the freedom of capital movements, financial markets would penalize undisciplined budgetary behavior with higher interest rates and thus create pressure for convergence toward sound fiscal policies. Other, more institutional arguments against binding budgetary rules were that in virtually all federally organized states (such as the United States, the Federal Republic of Germany, or Switzerland) the central authorities had no mandate to control the budget policies of the regional entities; to give an EC organ such as the Council of Ministers the power to decide on the budgetary policies of individual countries would infringe on the sovereignty of governments and parliaments of these countries and limit the democratic responsibility of elected political institutions.

On the other hand, it was stressed that in the EC—in contrast to federally organized countries—the central budget (the Community budget) was and would remain for quite some time much too small to have any macroeconomically significant impact. It was therefore on the level of national budgets that the coordinative action would be required. On the basis of past experience, however, not too much faith could be placed in effective voluntary coordination in the budget field. At the same time financial markets are not seen as effectively improving the budgetary discipline of divergent countries. Furthermore—it was argued—should a country run into serious budgetary problems, political pressure on other member countries was likely to develop and

a bail-out could not be excluded.[101] On this subject, the Delors Report (p.24) stated:

. . .experience suggests that market perceptions do not necessarily provide strong and compelling signals and that access to a large capital market may for some time even facilitate the financing of economic imbalances. Rather than leading to a gradual adaptation of borrowing costs, market views about the creditworthiness of official borrowers tend to change abruptly and result in the closure of access to market financing. The constraints imposed by market forces might either be too slow and weak or too sudden and disruptive.

The issue of democratic accountability, however, was recognized by the Delors Report; it should be solved on a political level, for example, by a more extended involvement of the European Parliament (pp. 39–40).

The debate summarized above centers mainly on the problem of coordinating budgetary policies insofar as they have a macroeconomic dimension. It is commonly agreed, however, that policies regarding the level and structure of expenditure and taxation, to the extent that they are compatible with overall macroeconomic requirements, should remain a prerogative of national authorities. A broadly held view seems to be that, as the internal market is being realized, market pressure would work toward a certain degree of harmonization of the structure and size of expenditures and taxes to avoid the emergence of distortions and the loss of competitiveness by countries with high tax levels.

Central Bank Independence

The question of independence for a future European central bank has also been widely discussed. (It may be better to talk in terms of "autonomy," since in a democratic society no central bank (or any other "independent" institution, such as courts) can be fully independent of elected political institutions, constitutional or other legal frameworks, or of public opinion.) At issue is whether a central bank should be "independent of instructions from national governments and Community authorities," as called for in the Delors Report (p.26), in carrying out its legally defined duties and in formulating and implementing its policies. It is not surprising that a number of senior central bank officials favor independence, arguing that only an inde-

[101] See, for example, Costa (1989), Szász (1988), and Pöhl (1990a). For a variety of views opposing binding rules, see Lawson in United Kingdom (1989a), Wissenschaftlicher Beirat beim Bundesministerium für Wirtschaft (1989a), and Bredenkamp and Deppler (1990). See also Commission of the European Communities (1990a and b), discussed below. For comments on the interrelation between monetary and fiscal policy under fixed exchange rates, see Guitián (1988), p. 13 and Schinasi (1989), p. 407.

pendent central bank could guarantee the primary objective of monetary policy—price stability—in a European economic and monetary union.[102]

The background to the debate is a basic conceptual difference in thinking about the framework and objectives of economic policy. On the one hand, there is the concept that all aspects of economic policy, including monetary policy, should be subject to a unified approach and be formulated, implemented, and made consistent by the government, which—through parliament—is answerable to the electorate. In this concept, price stability is only one—albeit often an important one—of several objectives of economic policy. It has to compete with other objectives such as economic growth, high employment, balance of payments equilibrium, exchange rate stability, and fairness in taxation. Under this concept, a shift in priorities can occur over time, and in many countries has actually occurred. In some countries, economic objectives other than price stability, particularly full employment, have been consistently given priority. It is only natural then to this line of thinking that a central bank should have only limited independence and in the extreme would not be much more than an executive branch of government in its particular field of expertise.

In the other concept, price stability is not seen as only one of several objectives of economic policy. It is rather considered an essential, quasiconstitutional part of the basic framework within which economic and social policy is conducted. It is regarded as a complement as well as being equal to other essential elements of the economic order of a country such as market economy principles, private property, and freedom to engage in domestic and international economic activity.[103] From this view derives the axiom for a high degree of independence for the central bank in some countries, such as Germany, Switzerland, and the United States.[104] While these central banks are independent in the pursuit of their tasks and their policies, they are not independent in the sense of being free of democratic control and outside the formation of opinion in society. Democratic control is exercised not by day-to-day intervention in policy formation but in the setting of the determinants of monetary policy: the laws governing central bank responsibilities and activities; appointment procedures for top officials; and regular reporting to parliament and to the public at large. These central banks are subject to intense public scrutiny and the effectiveness of their policies is highly dependent on public approval and an affirmative social consensus.

Nigel Lawson, British Chancellor of the Exchequer when the Delors Report was issued, emphasized the aspect of democratic accountability for a central bank, found it wanting in the proposals of the Delors Report, and concluded that it was for "these reasons of sovereignty and of democratic accountability that I reject the proposal [as embodied in the Delors Report] for economic and monetary union."[105] Karl Otto Pöhl, President of the Deutsche Bundesbank, saw democratic control as ensured if the European System of Central Banks "came about by an agreement between democratic governments, if the agreement were ratified by democratically elected parliaments and if the system were provided with a clearly defined mandate." He suggested that the members of the ESCB Board could be appointed by the EC Council of Ministers, and the Chairman of the ESCB would report regularly to the European Parliament.[106] Other proposals include the involvement of the European Parliament in the appointment of Board members and the submission of annual reports to the European Parliament, the Council of Ministers, and the EC Commission.[107] Also, comprehensive information for the general public that would allow control by public opinion and the financial community has been recommended.[108]

The Delors Report did not contain detailed proposals regarding accountability, but it did note the issue by recommending that the ESCB submit annual reports to the European Parliament and the European Council and that the Chairman of the ESCB be invited to report to these institutions (p.26). Generally, it appears that the issue is not whether there should be accountability but rather what form it would take.

Another dispute is whether, during the phase of transition to full EMU in which the ESCB would be set up

---

[102] See, for example, Ciampi (1989b); Duisenberg (1989b); Pöhl (1990a); Doyle (1990); de Larosière (1990a and b); Chalikias (1990). See also Giscard d'Estaing, as quoted in *Börsen-Zeitung*, February 17, 1990. On this issue, see also a recent statement of the Deutsche Bundesbank of September 19, 1990, in which the consequences of establishing EMU and the conditions for assuring monetary stability are discussed (Deutsche Bundesbank, *Monthly Report*, October 1990).

[103] This view is strongly reflected in the concept of *Ordnungspolitik* as developed by Walter Eucken and a number of Austrian, German, and Swiss economists. *Ordnungspolitik* could be defined as the underlying basic policy aimed at establishing and maintaining a certain economic order characterized by free markets, unrestricted competition, free international trade, and what has sometimes been called "nonpolitical money."

[104] In a study exploring the interconnections between politics and macroeconomics, Alesina (1989) found an inverse relationship between the degree of autonomy of a central bank and the inflation rate: among 17 industrialized countries, the 4 most independent central banks (Japan, the United States, and, especially, the Federal Republic of Germany and Switzerland) have been associated with four of the five lowest inflation rates (measured as an average for 1973–86).

[105] Before the Treasury and Civil Service Commission, June 12, 1989 (United Kingdom, 1989a).

[106] Pöhl (1990a).

[107] Szász (1988) and Ciampi (1989b). For an interesting discussion of the interrelationships between central bank independence, accountability, and the pursuit of price stability, see Blunden (1990).

[108] See Ciampi (1989b) and Pöhl (1990a).

(stage two of the Delors Report), national central banks should become more independent than at present. The underlying argument is that the ESCB would hardly be free of instructions from national authorities if various members of its supreme organ, the ESCB Council, could individually still be subject to such instructions. The Delors Report refers rather carefully to this problem (p.35). Others have addressed it more forcefully and requested full independence for the participating central banks before the implementation of a common monetary policy.[109]

Implementation of Stage One and Intergovernmental Conference on EMU

July 1, 1990 marked two important developments in financial and monetary integration in the EC: most member states had to liberalize all capital movements in line with the 1988 directive (see Section IV), and stage one, as envisaged in the proposals of the Delors Committee, of the process leading to EMU began.

As noted above, France and Italy had abolished their remaining capital restrictions ahead of schedule as of January 1 and May 14, 1990, respectively. Belgium-Luxembourg had ended their regime of a dual exchange market for current and capital transactions, due under the directive by the end of 1992, in March 1990. Other developments in 1989 and 1990 that helped to strengthen the EMS and the credibility of the exchange rate and monetary policies of various EMS countries were the decisions of Spain in June 1989 to join the ERM, availing itself of the option of wider fluctuation margins of ± 6 percent, and of Italy to adopt the narrow margins of ± 2.25 percent in January 1990. Also of interest in this context is the decision of the Belgian Government in June 1990 to tie the Belgian franc firmly to the deutsche mark. Furthermore, as of October 8, 1990, the United Kingdom has been participating in the ERM, also using the wider margins of ± 6 percent.

The preparations for stage one of the Delors Report started soon after the Madrid agreement of the European Council in June 1989. In March 1990, the EC Council of Ministers adopted amendments to key decisions to intensify cooperation in economic and monetary policies.[110] The 1974 decision on economic convergence was made more specific by referring explicitly to the achievement of "sustained non-inflationary growth, together with a high level of employment." According to the amended decision, the Council of

Ministers is to survey member countries' economies, applying the principles of price stability, sound public finances and monetary conditions, sound overall balances of payments, and open, competitive markets. The Council is to examine at least twice a year the economic conditions, prospects, and policies in the EC and its individual countries; the compatibility of policies within member countries and the EC; and the external economic environment and its interaction with the EC economy. The Council of Ministers will be assisted in its surveillance task by the EC Commission and the Monetary Committee. Together with the Commission, it shall report on the results of such surveillance to the European Council and the European Parliament.

The 1964 Council decision on cooperation between the EC central banks established the Committee of Central Bank Governors of the EC countries. The Committee's task was to hold consultations on monetary and exchange market policies and to exchange information about these policies at regular intervals. The amendment of March 1990 expanded and defined more precisely the mandate of the Committee. The tasks of the Committee now are

> to promote the coordination of the monetary policies of the Member States with the aim of achieving price stability as a necessary condition for the proper functioning of the European Monetary System and the realization of the objective of monetary stability; to formulate opinions on the overall orientation of monetary and exchange rate policy as well as on the respective measures introduced in individual Member States; to express opinions to individual governments and the Council of Ministers on policies which might affect the internal and external monetary situation in the Community and, in particular, the functioning of the European Monetary System. (Art. 3.)

Furthermore, the Committee is to prepare an annual report to be transmitted to the European Parliament, the Council of Ministers, and the European Council. The Chairman of the Committee may be invited to appear before the European Parliament and may be authorized by the Committee to make the outcome of its deliberations public.

Organizationally, the term of office of the Committee Chairman was extended from one to three years. The President of the Deutsche Bundesbank, Karl Otto Pöhl, was appointed to this office. The Committee also formed a Committee of Alternates, chaired by Jean-Jacques Rey from the National Bank of Belgium, and subcommittees for monetary policy, foreign exchange policy, and banking supervision. A secretariat and a small research unit have been formed, and a secretary-general has been appointed.

Since its reorganization, the Committee has been drafting the statutes for a future European System of

[109] See Wissenschaftlicher Beirat beim Bundesministerium für Wirtschaft (1989b), para. 3. See also *The Economist* (1989).
[110] OJ, L 78/23 and L 78/25, March 24, 1990.

Central Banks. An interesting question in this respect has been whether voting in the Council of the ESCB should be weighted to reflect the relative economic strength of individual countries or whether there should be the rule of "one member, one vote." In September 1990 the Committee's chairman presented an interim report on the statutes of a future European central bank, indicating agreement on a number of important points. The Committee will present a final report in time for the Intergovernmental Conference in December 1990. Another task the Committee has undertaken is to study the compatibility of monetary targets for the major EC currencies.

At its meeting in Strasbourg in December 1989, the European Council had called for an Intergovernmental Conference to prepare an amendment of the EEC Treaty with a view to the final stages of EMU. On April 28, 1990, the European Council, in a special meeting in Dublin, went one step further. It pronounced itself "satisfied with progress achieved so far towards establishing the single market without frontiers" and asked that the Intergovernmental Conference "conclude its work rapidly with the objective of ratification [of the Treaty amendment] by member states before the end of 1992," to coincide with the envisaged completion of the internal market. At its meeting on June 25–26, 1990, again in Dublin, the European Council agreed to open the Intergovernmental Conference on EMU in Rome in mid-December 1990, and to call at the same time an Intergovernmental Conference on Political Union, following an initiative by French President Mitterand and German Chancellor Kohl. Both conferences are scheduled to begin on December 14.

In addition to the work undertaken by the Committee of Central Bank Governors, other bodies of the EC have also begun to prepare for the Intergovernmental Conference on EMU. The Monetary Committee, consisting of senior officials of the finance ministries and central banks of EC countries and the EC Commission, has been discussing a number of important questions. Among these are the extent to which central and binding coordination rules are needed for budgetary policies to be consistent with a common monetary policy, and whether the final responsibility for exchange rate and exchange market intervention policy should rest with the political authorities or the ESCB. In this connection, it has been pointed out that monetary policy could not be divided into domestic and external components. On the other hand, it has been emphasized that in view of their general economic as well as political importance, exchange rate and intervention policies in many countries have been the prerogative of the political authorities. It is understood, however, that particularly in an international monetary system where major currencies float against each other, no obvious demar-

cation line exists between the more political decisions on the choice of exchange rate regime and parity changes and decisions with regard to day-to-day exchange rate developments and interventions in the foreign exchange market.

In March 1990, the EC Commission presented to the Council of Ministers a communication on economic and monetary union endorsing the general approach to EMU of the Delors Committee.[111] The Commission advocated the creation of the European System of Central Banks (nicknamed EuroFed); a high degree of independence for the ESCB from national governments and EC institutions; the objective of price stability; and the principle of subsidiarity. The Commission stated that a centralized economic policy was unnecessary but a sufficient degree of consistency was essential. The Commission deviated from the Delors Report in not calling for uniform binding *rules* on budgetary policy, arguing instead for binding *procedures*. The convergence of budgetary policies should mainly be sought by incorporating budgetary rules into *national* law and by the monitoring, adjustment, and enforcement of such strategies through regular mutual surveillance at the Community level. The Commission stressed that there was virtual agreement on two rules: no monetary financing of public deficits or priority access to markets for public authorities, and no bailing out (although this would not exclude ad hoc conditional assistance).

In preparation for the Intergovernmental Conference on EMU, the Commission has also undertaken a comprehensive appraisal of the likely economic effects—costs as well as benefits—of the move to EMU, and a report on these issues has been published.[112]

Other highly political issues were also extensively discussed. One relates to the number of stages needed to achieve EMU. The Delors Report had proposed three. In stage two, policy coordination was to be further intensified and the ESCB set up, without yet assuming full responsibility for a common monetary policy. Whether a second stage was needed or desirable has been debated. It has been argued that after successful completion of the first stage, with an effective coordination of economic and monetary policies and a high degree of economic convergence in place, one should move directly to the third stage, that is, to monetary union. The ESCB would then take on all its responsibilities and not remain in a waiting position during which it would be difficult to acquire credibility. Others hold that problems of transition to the final stage were given short shrift in the Delors Report: the basic concept of

---

[111] Commission of the European Communities (1990b).
[112] Commission of the European Communities, "One Market, One Money," *European Economy*, No. 44 (Brussels), October 1990. See *IMF Survey*, November 26, 1990. ·

a common monetary policy had not been sufficiently detailed nor had the instruments necessary to assure the integration of the ESCB with the national central banks and to implement a common monetary policy been specified. These problems would have to be addressed in stage two.[113]

Another issue that has attracted attention and created some controversy was whether EMU could and should be started by those EC countries that politically and economically were ready for such a move, with other countries joining later. Such a two-speed procedure would allow a core of EC countries, which have achieved a high degree of price and cost convergence, to move ahead in forming the union; references were made to a group consisting of Belgium, France, Germany, Luxembourg, and the Netherlands as well as Denmark and Ireland. Other countries would join as soon as they were ready, in particular in terms of inflation and budget performance. As noted in Section III, substantial divergences of performance still exist between not only EC but also ERM countries. It was pointed out that in a number of areas such as the liberalization of capital movements or participation in all aspects of the EMS, not all EC countries have advanced at the same speed. Others stressed, however, that such a procedure would be damaging to the coherence and further development of the EC in economic as well as in political terms.

On September 8 and 9, 1990, the economics and finance ministers and the central bank governors of the EC countries met in Rome to discuss problems of EMU. The EC Commission presented a paper that proposed starting stage two of the process leading to EMU on January 1, 1993 and moving to the third and final stage "soon after." Belgium, Denmark, France, and Italy supported this time plan while several other countries, including Germany, Luxembourg, the Netherlands, as well as Greece, Ireland, Portugal, and Spain were in favor of a more measured pace. At the European Council meeting of October 27–28, 1990, in Rome, the EC countries, with the exception of the United Kingdom, agreed to begin stage two on January 1, 1994, subject, inter alia, to further advances in economic and monetary integration as well as "further lasting and satisfactory progress towards real and monetary convergence." They also agreed to establish at the beginning of this stage a new monetary institution for the EC, comprising member states' central banks and a central organ.[114]

It will be up to the Intergovernmental Conference on EMU to resolve or at least identify possible solutions to the various issues under discussion. They encompass institutional and technical problems: how the ESCB should be organized and operate, the scope of its responsibilities, and the degree of its independence from political interference. There are problems with economic and political significance: they relate to the speed of the process of monetary integration and the contentious issue of a possible "two-speed" process. Also, the question of the extent to which monetary and economic union should be developed simultaneously and at a similar pace is at the heart of the dispute about binding coordination procedures for budgetary policies. Ultimately, the debate is about the question of whether, when, and to what extent countries will be ready to surrender sovereignty in the economic and in the last analysis the political field to common institutions and to share in a common decision-making process.

---

[113] For some aspects of this discussion, see Bofinger (1990) and Ungerer (1990b).

[114] For details, see the communiqué of the European Council meeting (Appendix II).

Appendix I
Statistical Tables

Table 1. EMS: Periods of Strain[1]

No.	Period	Source of Strain	Signaled by Divergence indicator[2]	Signaled by Parity grid	Remedies Adopted
1	May–June 1979	D: Widening CA deficits and deficient capital inflow. B: Continued lack of confidence.	DKr: −75	DM/BF	Intervention to support both BF and DKr. B: Discount rate up from 6 to 9 percent. D: Discount rate up from 8 to 9 percent.
2	Aug.–Sept. 1979	D and B: Capital inflows induced by earlier increases in nominal interest rates dry out in both countries.	DKr: −75 BF: −75	DM/DKr	Intervention to support both BF and DKr. D: Discount rate up from 9 to 11 percent on 9/17, after which intervention stops. B: Discount rate up from 9 to 10 percent. Realignment 1: DM up, DKr down relative to other EMS currencies.
3	Nov. 1979	Uncertainty after parliamentary election in late October puts pressure on the DKr.	DKr: slightly negative few days before realignment		Intervention in support of DKr. Realignment 2: DKr devalued against all other EMS currencies.
4	Dec. 1979– March 1980	D: Deficient capital inflow because of uncertainty about DKr in view of two recent realignments and because of increasing international nominal interest rates. B: Deficient capital inflow to finance CA deficits.		FF/BF (in March)	Intervention keeps DKr in the middle of the band. Discount rate up from 11 to 13 percent. B: Intervention majority in EMS currencies to support BF. Discount rate up from 10 to 14 percent.
5	Oct. 1980	G: Weak CA position relative to U.S. and major EMS countries plus interest differential disfavoring DM-denominated investments.	DM: −70	FF/DM	Intervention in support of DM. F: Loosening of credit market. G: Slight tightening of credit market.
6	Feb. 1981	G: As U.S. interest rates surge and uncertainty about G's strategic (Poland) and economic position increases, pressure on DM becomes heavy.	DM: −60s FF: touching +75 occasionally in Jan. and Feb.	FF/BF and FF/BF	Intervention in $ and FF to support DM. G: Special Lombard rate introduced; substantial tightening of monetary policy.
7	March 1981	BF and Lit exposed at bottom of band after DM firming. After devaluation of Lit, BF still under heavy pressure.	BF: −75 Lit: −75 (briefly)	DM/BF and FF/BF	I: Intervention followed by increase in discount rate from 16.5 to 19 percent. Realignment 3: Devaluation of Lit. B: Intervention followed by increase in discount rate from 12 to 16 percent.
8	May 1981	Presidential election in France (5/10/81)	FF: −75 (two weeks from 5/11/81)	DM/FF	F: Intervention. Interest rate and exchange control measures.
9	Aug.–Sept. 1981	On the background of pessimism about devaluation of the FF, DM gains strength on improving external performance, and FF and BF have problems following DM up against $.	DM: +75 (last two weeks of Sept.). BF: not past −75 but most "diverging" of weak currencies.	DM/BF	Intervention in support of weak EMS currencies. Realignment 4: DM and f. revalued, and FF and Lit devalued against DKr, BF, £Ir.

Table 1 *(continued).* **EMS: Periods of Strain[1]**

No.	Period	Source of Strain	Signaled by		Remedies Adopted
			Divergence indicator[2]	Parity grid	
10	Nov. 1981	Brief pressure on BF when negotiations to form a government break down.	BF: once below −75 on 12/10.		Intervention in support of BF. B: Discount rate up from 13 to 15 percent.
11	Feb. 1982	Diminishing confidence in future performance of Belgian economy.	BF: close to, but not past −75 DKr: slightly negative		B: Intervention. Realignment 5: Devaluation of BF and DKr against other EMS currencies.
12	March 1982	F: Widening inflation differential with G. DKr and BF lose strength acquired in previous realignments.	FF: one flash (−76) on 3/23; otherwise well within bounds.	DM/FF and f./FF	F: Intervention, tightening of monetary policy, exchange controls, budget.
13	May–June 1982	"The weekend syndrome": pressure on BF, FF, Lit, especially late in week. Persistent realignment rumors.	DM: above +75 from end-April. BF: most "diverging" currency at bottom	DM/BF	Intervention. Realignment 6: Revaluation of DM and f. and devaluation of Lit and FF against DKr, BF, and £Ir.
14	Dec. 1982– March 1983	Deteriorating trade balance and inflation in France. Increasing pressure on FF, especially late in week; persistent realignment rumors; anticipation of realignment after March elections in G and F.	BF: frequently below in January, February; FF: below in March	DM/FF f./BF	Substantial intervention in support of BF and FF, interest rate measures in B, G, and N. Emergency foreign exchange measures in B. Realignment 7: Revaluation of DM, f., DKr, BF, and devaluation of FF, Lit, £Ir.
15	March–July 1985	Significant deterioration in performance of Italian economy in fiscal and external accounts puts Lit under pressure.	Lit: −40 Movement of lira to the lower part of the wide band.	DKr/Lit	Realignment 8: Devaluation of Lit by about 8 percent against other participating currencies.
16	Dec. 1985– Jan. 1986	Weak performance of Italian and Belgian economies and realignment rumors; decline of sterling against participating currencies.	Ir: From 0 to −60 BF: −75 Drop of Ir to bottom of narrow band; further downward pressure on BF; decline of Lit from its strong position after realignment 8.	DM/BF	Substantial intervention in support of BF; increase in Belgian and Irish interest rates; tightening on monetary policy and foreign exchange restrictions in Italy.
17	April 4, 1986	F: Widening inflation differential particularly with G; realignment initiated by new government.	FF and Ir fall below their lower intervention limits, DM and f. rise above their upper intervention limits.	. . .	Realignment 9: Revaluation of DM, f., BF, and DKr; devaluation of FF.
18	Aug. 2, 1986	Ire: Depreciation of $ and sterling against ERM currencies endangers competitive position of Irish economy.	Ir: from 16 to −37	FF/DKr	Realignment 10: Devaluation of £Ir by about 8 percent against other participating currencies.
19	January 12, 1987	Continued $ weakness. FF under stress partly linked to difficulties in wage negotiations. DM at highest levels against $ since October 1980.	FF falls to its lower intervention limit against DM. DM: +75 to −30 FF: −60 to +30		Realignment 11: Intervention, increase in interest rates in France, and subsequent realignment. DM, f., BF revalued against FF and other ERM currencies.
20	October 1987	Sharp drop in U.S. stock market prices and resulting depreciation of $.	FF allowed to depreciate within the band against DM.		Coordinated intervention, interest rate adjustments, and more extended use of available fluctuation margin in ERM.
21	late Aug./ early Sept. 1988	Sharp drop in value of $.			Intervention by Bank of France and Bank of Italy to support FF and Lit. Bundesbank raised discount rate by ½ percent to 3.5 percent, Bank of France raised its money market intervention rate from 6.75 to 7 percent; similar upward moves made in U.K., Belgium, and Netherlands. Continued sale of dollars by central banks after interest rate increases in efforts to maintain dollar's downward momentum.

Table 1 *(concluded).* EMS: Periods of Strain[1]

No.	Period	Source of Strain	Signaled by		Remedies Adopted
			Divergence indicator[2]	Parity grid	
22	January 8, 1990	Significant strengthening of DM in latter part of 1989 linked to political developments in Eastern Europe. Downward move of Lit in preceding weeks, particularly against DM.			Realignment 12: Lit devalued by 3.7 percent. Lit placed in narrow 2.25 percent fluctuation band.

Source: Fund staff estimates and calculations.

[1]Defined as periods with reports of substantial interference in the exchange market by intervention, capital and exchange controls, or measures of monetary policy motivated by exchange rate developments. Notation: B-Belgium; BF-Belgian franc; D-Denmark; DKr-Danish krone; F-France; FF-French franc; G-Federal Republic of Germany; DM-deutsche mark; Ire-Ireland; £Ir-Irish pound; I-Italy; Lit-Italian lira; N-Netherlands; f.-Netherlands guilder; U.S.-United States: $-U.S. dollar; CA-current account.

[2]The divergence indicator shows the movement of the exchange rate of each ERM currency against the (weighted) average movement of the other ERM currencies. The criterion used is the divergence of the actual daily rate of the ERM currency, expressed in ECUs, from its ECU central rate. Adjustments are made for those currencies contained in the ECU but not participating in the ERM and the wider margins observed by the Italian lira. A currency crossing a "threshold of convergence," set at 75 percent of the maximum divergence spread, raises the presumption that the authorities concerned will take corrective action. In practice, this provision has played only a limited role. For more details, see Ungerer, Evans, and Nyberg (1983), p. 15.

Table 2. EMS: Economic Measures in Connection with Realignments

Realignment Date	Realignment Wording Based on Official Communiqué	Major Measures in			
		Belgium	Denmark	France	Italy
September 24, 1979	Shift in cross rate between the deutsche mark and the Danish krone of 5 percent. Shift in cross rate between the deutsche mark and other EMS currencies of 2 percent.	—	—	—	—
November 30, 1979	Devaluation of the Danish krone by 5 percent against other EMS currencies (no communiqué).	—	Energy component removed from wage-regulating index. Short-term price and wage freeze measures. Increases in direct personal wealth and corporate taxes.	—	—
March 23, 1981	Devaluation of Italian lira by 6 percent against other EMS currencies.	—	—	—	Discount rate up 2 1/2 percent to 19 percent. Government spending cut plans.
October 5, 1981	Revaluation of the deutsche mark and the Netherlands guilder by 5.5 percent against the Danish krone, the Belgian franc, the Luxembourg franc, and the Irish pound. Devaluation of the French franc and the Italian lira by 3 percent against the Danish krone, the Belgian franc, and the Irish pound.	—	—	Temporary price and profit freeze. Incomes policy aiming at maintenance of average income purchasing power, narrowing of income range. F 10.15 billion government expenditure in suspense.	—
February 22, 1982	Devaluation of the Belgian franc and the Luxembourg franc by 8.5 percent and the Danish krone by 3 percent against other EMS currencies.	Temporary freeze of wages and longer-run measures to impede complete wage indexation. Temporary price freeze. Reduction in corporate tax burden. Measures to stimulate the stock market.	—	—	—
June 14, 1982	Change in bilateral rates: between the French franc and the deutsche mark, f.: 10 percent; between the Italian lira and the deutsche mark, f.: 7 percent; between the Danish krone, the Belgian franc, the Luxembourg franc, the Irish pound, and the deutsche mark, f.: 4.25 percent.	—	—	Temporary freeze of wages, prices, rents, and dividends (except minimum wage) to be followed up by agreements on price and dividend behavior and indexation practices for wages. Revision of 1983 budget to restrict deficit to F 120 billion (3 percent of GNP).	Announcement of budgetary austerity measures, June 23.

53

Table 2 (concluded).   EMS: Economic Measures in Connection with Realignments

Realignment Date	Realignment Wording Based on Official Communiqué	Major Measures in			
		Belgium	Denmark	France	Italy

March 21, 1983	Change in central rates
	deutsche mark +5.5
	Netherlands
	  guilder +3.5
	Danish krone +2.5
	Belgian franc +1.5
	Luxembourg
	  franc +1.5
	French franc −2.5
	Italian lira −2.5
	Irish pound −3.5
		—	—	Package of restrictive measures in budgetary, monetary, and foreign exchange fields.	—

July 20, 1985	Change in central rates
	Irish pound +2
	French franc +2
	Danish krone +2
	Netherlands
	  guilder +2
	deutsche mark +2
	Belgian franc +2
	Luxembourg
	  franc +2
	Italian lira −6
		—	—	—	Announcement of a package of revenue-raising measures aimed at containing an increase in the fiscal deficit over the target for 1985. Modification of the wage indexation mechanism (*scala mobile*).

April 6, 1986	Change in central rates
	deutsche mark +3
	Netherlands
	  guilder +3
	Belgian franc +1
	Luxembourg
	  franc +1
	Danish krone +1
	Irish pound 0
	Italian lira 0
	French franc −3
		—	—	Steps to slow nominal wage growth and to reduce the government budget deficit. The noninterest component of the deficit to be eliminated in the course of the next three years. The target to contain the growth of M3 below 5 percent in 1986 was reasserted. Relaxation of exchange controls.	—

August 2, 1986	Devaluation of the Irish pound by 8 percent vis-à-vis all other participating currencies.	—	—	—	—

January 12, 1987	Change in central rates
	Belgian franc +2
	Luxembourg
	  franc +2
	deutsche mark +3
	Netherlands
	  guilder +3
				No specific policy measures in support of the realignment were announced, but the ministers and governors asked the Monetary Committee and the Committee of Central Bank Governors to examine measures to strengthen the operating mechanism of the EMS.	

January 8, 1990	Change in central rates Italian lira −3.7 Incorporation of the lira in the narrow 2.25 percent fluctuation band of the ERM.				Italian authorities pledge to maintain the budget deficit within forecast limits and encourage a swifter reduction in inflation.

Sources: Commission of the European Communities, and Fund staff calculations.

Table 3. EMS Realignments: Percentage Changes in Bilateral Central Rates[1]

	Sept. 24, 1979	Nov. 30, 1979	Mar. 23, 1981	Oct. 5, 1981	Feb. 22, 1982	June 14, 1982	Mar. 21, 1983	July 22, 1985	April 7, 1986	Aug. 4, 1986	Jan. 12, 1987	Jan. 8, 1990
Belgian and Luxembourg francs					−8.5		+1.5	+2.0	+1.0		+2.0	
Danish krone	−2.9	−4.8			−3.0		+2.5	+2.0	+1.0			
Deutsche mark	+2.0			+5.5		+4.25	+5.5	+2.0	+3.0		+3.0	
French franc				−3.0		−5.75	−2.5	+2.0	−3.0			
Italian lira			−6.0	−3.0		−2.75	−2.5	−6.0				−3.7
Irish pound							−3.5	+2.0		−8.0		
Netherlands guilder				+5.5		+4.25	+3.5	+2.0	+3.0		+3.0	

Sources: Commission of the European Communities and Fund staff calculations.

[1]Calculated as the percentage change against the group of currencies whose bilateral parities remained unchanged in the realignment, except for the realignments (Mar. 21, 1983, July 22, 1985) in which all currencies were realigned. For these the percentages are shown as in the official communiqué.

Table 4. EMS: Bilateral Central Rates[1]

Currency Units	100 Belgian/ Luxembourg Francs	100 Danish Kroner	100 Deutsche Mark	100 French Francs	100 Italian Lire	100 Irish Pounds	100 Netherlands Guilders	100 Spanish Pesetas	100 Pounds Sterling
Belgian/Luxembourg francs									
Mar. 13, 1979		556.852	1,571.64	680.512	3.43668	5,954.71	1,450.26		
Sept. 24, 1979		540.942	1,603.07	680.512	3.43668	5,954.71	1,450.26		
Nov. 30, 1979		515.186	1,603.07	680.512	3.43668	5,954.71	1,450.26		
Mar. 23, 1981		515.186	1,603.07	680.512	3.23048	5,954.71	1,450.26		
Oct. 5, 1981		515.186	1,691.25	660.097	3.13355	5,954.71	1,530.03		
Feb. 22, 1982		546.154	1,848.37	721.415	3.42466	6,507.92	1,672.16		
June 14, 1982		546.154	1,926.93	679.941	3.33047	6,507.92	1,743.23		
Mar. 21, 1983		551.536	2,002.85	653.144	3.19922	6,187.32	1,777.58		
July 22, 1985		551.536	2,002.85	653.144	2.94831	6,187.32	1,777.58		
Apr. 7, 1986		551.536	2,042.52	627.278	2.19120	6,126.06	1,812.78		
Aug. 4, 1986		551.536	2,042.52	627.278	2.19120	5,635.98	1,812.78		
Jan. 12, 1987		540.723	2,062.55	614.977	2.86187	5,525.45	1,830.54	—	
Jan. 8, 1990		540.723	2,062.55	614.977	2.75661	5,525.45	1,830.54	31.7316	
Oct. 8, 1990		540.723	2,062.55	614.977	2.75661	5,525.45	1,830.54	31.7316	6,084.51
Danish kroner									
Mar. 13, 1979	17.9581		282.237	122.207	0.617161	1,069.35	260.439		
Sept. 24, 1979	18.4862		296.348	125.801	0.635312	1,100.81	268.098		
Nov. 30, 1979	19.4105		311.165	132.091	0.667078	1,155.84	281.503		
Mar. 23, 1981	19.4105		311.165	132.091	0.627052	1,155.84	281.503		
Oct. 5, 1981	19.4105		328.279	128.128	0.60824	1,155.84	296.986		
Feb. 22, 1982	18.3098		338.433	132.09	0.62705	1,191.59	306.171		
June 14, 1982	18.3098		352.817	124.496	0.609804	1,191.59	319.183		
Mar. 21, 1983	18.1312		363.141	118.423	0.580057	1,121.84	322.297		
July 22, 1985	18.1312		363.141	118.423	0.534563	1,121.84	322.297		
Apr. 7, 1986	18.1312		370.332	113.732	0.529268	1,110.72	328.676		
Aug. 4, 1986	18.1312		370.332	113.732	0.529268	1,021.86	328.676		
Jan. 12, 1987	18.4938		381.443	113.732	0.529268	1,021.86	338.537	—	
Jan. 8, 1990	18.4938		381.443	113.732	0.509803	1,021.86	338.537	5.86837	
Oct. 8, 1990	18.4938		381.443	113.732	0.509803	1,021.86	338.537	5.86837	1,125.26
Deutsche mark									
Mar. 13, 1979	6.36277	35.4313		43.2995	0.218668	378.886	92.2767		
Sept. 24, 1979	6.238	33.7441		42.4505	0.21438	371.457	90.4673		
Nov. 30, 1979	6.238	32.1373		42.4505	0.21438	371.457	90.4673		
Mar. 23, 1981	6.238	32.1373		42.4505	0.201518	371.457	90.4673		
Oct. 5, 1981	5.9128	30.4619		39.0302	0.185281	352.09	90.4673		
Feb. 22, 1982	5.41018	29.5479		39.0302	0.185281	353.09	90.4673		
June 14, 1982	5.18961	28.3433		35.2863	0.172839	337.736	90.4673		
Mar. 21, 1983	4.99288	27.5375		32.6107	0.159733	308.925	88.7526		
July 22, 1985	4.99288	27.5375		32.6107	0.147205	308.925	88.7526		
Apr. 7, 1986	4.8959	27.0028		30.7109	0.142917	299.926	88.7526		
Aug. 4, 1986	4.8959	27.0028		30.7109	0.142917	275.934	88.7526		
Jan. 12, 1987	4.84837	26.2162		29.8164	0.138754	267.894	88.7526	—	
Jan. 8, 1990	4.84837	26.2162		29.8164	0.133651	267.894	88.7526	1.53847	
Oct. 8, 1990	4.84837	26.2162		29.8164	0.133651	267.894	88.7526	1.53847	295.000
French francs									
Mar. 13, 1979	14.6948	81.8286	230.95		0.505013	875.034	213.113		
Sept. 24, 1979	14.6948	79.4905	235.568		0.505013	875.034	213.113		
Nov. 30, 1979	14.6948	75.7054	235.568		0.505013	875.034	213.113		
Mar. 23, 1981	14.6948	75.7054	235.568		0.474714	875.034	213.113		
Oct. 5, 1981	15.1493	78.047	256.212		0.474714	902.098	231.789		
Feb. 22, 1982	13.8616	75.706	256.212		0.474714	902.098	231.789		
June 14, 1982	14.7072	80.3239	283.396		0.489818	957.129	256.38		
Mar. 21, 1983	15.3106	84.4432	306.648		0.489819	947.313	272.158		
July 22, 1985	15.3106	84.4432	306.648		0.451402	947.313	272.158		
Apr. 7, 1986	15.9419	87.9257	325.617		0.465362	976.610	288.991		
Aug. 4, 1986	15.9419	87.9257	325.617		0.465362	898.480	288.991		
Jan. 12, 1987	16.2608	87.9257	335.386		0.465362	898.480	297.661	—	
Jan. 8, 1990	16.2608	87.9257	335.386		0.448247	898.480	297.661	5.15981	
Oct. 8, 1990	16.2608	87.9257	335.386		0.448247	898.480	297.661	5.15981	989.389

Table 4 (concluded). EMS: Bilateral Central Rates[1]

Currency Units	100 Belgian/ Luxembourg Francs	100 Danish Kroner	100 Deutsche Mark	100 French Francs	100 Italian Lire	100 Irish Pounds	100 Netherlands Guilders	100 Spanish Pesetas	100 Pounds Sterling
Italian lire									
Mar. 13, 1979	2,909.79	16,303.3	45,731.4	19,801.5		173,270.0	42,199.5		
Sept. 24, 1979	2,909.79	15,740.3	46,646.0	19,801.5		173,270.0	42,199.5		
Nov. 30, 1979	2,909.79	14,990.7	46,646.0	19,801.5		173,270.0	42,199.5		
Mar. 23, 1981	3,095.51	15,947.6	49,623.2	21,065.3		184,329.0	44,893.0		
Oct. 5, 1981	3,191.26	16,440.9	53,972.2	21,065.3		190,031.0	48,827.2		
Feb. 22, 1982	2,920.0	15,947.70	53,927.2	21,065.3		190,031.0	48,827.2		
June 14, 1982	3,002.58	16,398.7	57,857.4	20,415.7		195,405.0	52,341.9		
Mar. 21, 1983	3,125.76	17,239.7	62,604.3	20,415.7		193,401.0	55,563.0		
July 22, 1985	3,191.77	18,706.9	67,932.5	22,153.2		209,860.8	60,291.5		
Apr. 7, 1986	3,425.70	18,894.0	69,970.6	21,488.6		209,860.8	62,100.2		
Aug. 4, 1986	3,425.70	18,894.0	69,970.6	21,488.6		193,071.0	62,100.2		
Jan. 12, 1987	3,494.21	18,894.0	72,069.9	21,488.6		193,071.0	63,963.1	—	
Jan. 8, 1990	3,627.64	19,615.4	74,821.7	22,309.1		200,443.0	66,405.3	1,151.11	
Oct. 8, 1990	3,627.64	19,615.4	74,821 7	22,309.1		200,443.0	66,405.3	1,151.11	220.725
Irish pounds									
Mar. 13, 1979	1.67934	9.35146	26.3932	11.4281	0.0577136		24.3548		
Sept. 24, 1979	1.67934	9.08424	26.921	11.4281	0.0577136		24.3548		
Nov. 30, 1979	1.67934	8.65169	26.921	11.4281	0.0577136		24.3548		
Mar. 23, 1981	1.67934	8.65169	26.921	11.4281	0.0542508		24.3548		
Oct. 5, 1981	1.67934	8.65169	28.4018	11.0853	0.052623		25.6944		
Feb. 22, 1982	1.53659	8.39216	28.4018	11.0853	0.052623		25.6944		
June 14, 1982	1.53659	8.39216	29.6090	10.4479	0.05111758		26.7864		
Mar. 21, 1983	1.61621	8.91396	32.3703	10.5562	0.0517061		28.7295		
July 22, 1985	1.61621	8.91396	32.3703	10.5562	0.0476508		28.7295		
Apr. 7, 1986	1.63237	9.00315	33.3416	10.2395	0.0476508		29.5912		
Aug. 4, 1986	1.77431	9.78604	36.2405	11.1299	0.0517943		32.1644		
Jan. 12, 1987	1.80981	9.78604	37.3281	11.1299	0.0517943		33.1293	—	
Jan. 8, 1990	1.80981	9.78604	37.3281	11.1299	0.0498895		33.1293	0.574281	
Oct. 8, 1990	1.80981	9.87604	37.3281	11.1299	0.0498895		33.1293	0.574281	110.118
Netherlands guilders									
Mar. 13, 1979	6.89531	38.3967	108.37	46.9235	0.23697	410.597			
Sept. 24, 1979	6.89531	37.2998	110.537	46.9235	0.23697	410.597			
Nov. 30, 1979	6.89531	35.5237	110.537	46.9235	0.23697	410.597			
Mar. 23, 1981	6.89531	35.5237	110.537	46.9235	0.222752	410.597			
Oct. 5, 1981	6.53583	33.6716	110.537	43.1428	0.204804	389.19			
Feb. 22, 1982	5.98027	32.6615	110.537	43.1428	0.204804	389.190			
June 14, 1982	5.73646	31.3300	110.537	39.0045	0.191051	373.324			
Mar. 21, 1983	5.62561	31.0273	112.673	36.7434	0.179976	348.075			
July 22, 1985	5.62561	31.0273	112.673	36.7434	0.165861	348.075			
Apr. 7, 1986	5.51640	30.4251	112.673	34.6032	0.161030	337.938			
Aug. 4, 1986	5.51640	30.4251	112.673	34.6032	0.161030	310.903			
Jan. 12, 1987	5.46286	29.5389	112.673	33.5953	0.156340	301.848		—	
Jan. 8, 1990	5.46286	29.5389	112.673	33.5953	0.150590	301.848		1.73345	
Oct. 8, 1990	5.46286	29.5389	112.673	33.5953	0.150590	301.848		1.73345	332.389
Spanish pesetas									
Jan. 8, 1990[2]	315.143	1,704.05	6,500.0	1,938.06	8.68726	17,413.1	5,768.83		
Oct. 8, 1990	315.143	1,704.05	6,500.0	1,938.06	8.68726	17,413.1	5,768.83		19,175.0
Sterling									
Oct. 8, 1990	1.64352	8.88687	33.8984	10.1073	0.0426690	90.8116	30.0853	0.521514	

Sources: Commission of the European Communities and Fund staff calculations.

[1]Expressed as the price of 100 units of the currency on top of the column in the currency in the stub.

[2]The bilateral central rates for the Spanish peseta on June 19, 1989, the date of its entry into the ERM, are the same as those listed here, except for the rate vis-à-vis the Italian lira, which stood at 9.01899 on that date.

Table 5. EMS: ECU Central Rates[1]

	Mar. 13, 1979	Sept. 24, 1979	Nov. 30, 1979	Mar. 23, 1981	Oct. 5, 1981	Feb. 22, 1982	June 14, 1982	Mar. 21, 1983	July 22, 1985[2]	Apr. 7, 1986	Aug. 4, 1986	Jan. 12, 1987	Jan. 8, 1990	Oct. 8, 1990
Belgian/Luxembourg franc														
Units of national currency per ECU	39.4582	39.8456	39.7897	40.7985	40.7572	44.6963	44.9704	44.3662	44.8320	43.6761	43.1139	42.4582	42.1679	42.4032
Percentage change from previous central rate		0.98	-0.14	2.54	-0.10	9.66	0.61	-1.34	-0.15	-2.58	-1.29	-1.52	-0.68	0.56
Percentage change from initial central rate		0.98	0.84	3.40	3.29	13.28	13.97	12.44	13.62	10.69	9.26	7.60	6.87	7.46
Danish krone														
Units of national currency per ECU	7.08592	7.36594	7.72336	7.91917	7.91117	8.18382	8.2340	8.04412	8.12857	7.91896	7.81701	7.85212	7.79845	7.84195
Percentage change from previous central rate		3.95	4.85	2.54	-0.10	3.45	0.61	-2.31	-0.15	-2.58	-1.29	0.45	-0.68	0.56
Percentage change from initial central rate		3.95	9.00	11.76	11.65	15.49	16.20	13.52	14.71	11.76	10.32	10.81	10.06	10.67
Deutsche mark														
Units of national currency per ECU	2.51064	2.48557	2.48208	2.54502	2.40989	2.41815	2.33379	2.21515	2.23840	2.13834	2.11083	2.05853	2.04446	2.05586
Percentage change from previous central rate		-1.00	-0.1	2.54	-5.31	0.34	-3.48	-5.08	-0.15	-4.47	-1.29	-2.48	-0.68	0.56
Percentage change from initial central rate		-1.00	-0.1	1.37	-4.01	-3.68	-7.04	-11.77	-10.84	-14.83	-15.92	-18.01	-18.57	-18.11
French franc														
Units of national currency per ECU	5.79831	5.85522	5.84700	5.99526	6.17443	6.19564	6.61387	6.79271	6.86402	6.9628	6.87316	6.90403	6.85684	6.89509
Percentage change from previous central rate		0.98	-0.14	2.54	2.99	0.34	6.75	2.70	-0.15	1.44	-1.29	0.45	-0.68	0.56
Percentage change from initial central rate		0.98	0.84	3.40	6.49	6.85	14.07	17.15	18.38	20.08	18.54	19.07	18.26	18.92
Italian lira														
Units of national currency per ECU	1,148.15	1,159.42	1,157.79	1,262.92	1,300.13	1,305.13	1,350.27	1,386.78	1,520.60	1,496.21	1,476.95	1,483.58	1,529.70	1,538.24
Percentage change from previous central rate		0.98	-0.14	9.1	2.99	0.34	3.46	2.70	8.34	-1.60	-1.29	0.45	3.11	0.56
Percentage change from initial central rate		0.98	0.84	10.00	13.28	13.67	17.60	20.78	32.44	30.31	28.64	29.21	33.23	33.98
Irish pound														
Units of national currency per ECU	0.662638	0.669141	0.668201	0.685145	0.684452	0.686799	0.691011	0.71705	0.724578	0.712956	0.764976	0.768411	0.763159	0.767417
Percentage change from previous central rate		0.98	-0.14	2.54	-0.10	0.34	0.61	3.77	-0.15	-1.60	7.30	0.45	-0.680	0.56
Percentage change from initial central rate		0.98	0.84	3.40	3.29	3.65	4.28	8.21	9.35	7.59	15.44	15.96	15.17	15.81
Netherlands guilder														
Units of national currency per ECU	2.72077	2.74748	2.74362	2.81318	2.66382	2.57971	2.49587	2.49587	2.52208	2.40935	2.37833	2.31943	2.30358	2.31643
Percentage change from previous central rate		0.98	-0.14	2.54	-5.31	0.34	-3.49	-3.25	-0.15	-4.47	-1.29	-2.48	-0.68	0.56
Percentage change from initial central rate		0.98	0.84	3.40	-2.09	-1.76	-5.18	-8.27	-7.30	-11.45	-12.59	-14.75	-15.33	-14.86

Spanish peseta																				
Units of national currency per ECU	133.804[3]	—	—	—	—	—	—	—	—	—	—	—	—	—	—	—	—	—	132.889	133.631
Percentage change from previous central rate	—	—	—	—	—	—	—	—	—	—	—	—	—	—	—	—	—	—	−0.68	0.56
Percentage change from initial rate	—	—	—	—	—	—	—	—	—	—	—	—	—	—	—	—	—	—	−0.68	−0.13
Sterling																				
Units of national currency per ECU	—	—	—	—	—	—	—	—	—	—	—	—	—	—	—	—	—	—	—	0.696904
Percentage change from previous central rate	—	—	—	—	—	—	—	—	—	—	—	—	—	—	—	—	—	—	—	—
Percentage change from initial rate	—	—	—	—	—	—	—	—	—	—	—	—	—	—	—	—	—	—	—	—

Source: Commission of the European Communities.

[1] The change of any central rate expressed in terms of ECUs implies a simultaneous change of all other ECU central rates, because the ECU is made up of a basket of currencies. Positive sign indicates depreciation relative to the ECU.

[2] Percentage change from central rate as of May 1983, when the notional central rate of sterling was revalued and the other central rates devalued as part of a package to arrive at new common agricultural prices. No change in bilateral central rates and intervention limits of participating currencies occurred at this time.

[3] On June 19, 1989, the date of entry into the ERM.

Table 6. Deutsche Mark Interventions in the EMS

(In billions of deutsche mark)

		Obligatory	Intramarginal	Total	In Fed. Rep. of Germany[1]
By calendar years					
1979[2]	Purchases	—	−2.7	−2.7	−2.4
	Sales	+3.6	+8.1	+11.7	+11.7
	Balance	+3.6	+5.4	+9.0	+9.2
1980	Purchases	−5.9	−5.9	−11.8	−11.1
	Sales	—	+1.0	+1.0	+0.6
	Balance	−5.9	−4.9	−10.8	−10.5
1981	Purchases	−2.3	−8.1	−10.4	−11.6
	Sales	+17.3	+12.8	+30.1	+25.3
	Balance	+15.0	+4.7	+19.7	+13.7
1982	Purchases	—	−9.4	−9.4	−2.5
	Sales	+3.0	+12.8	+15.8	+6.1
	Balance	+3.0	+3.4	+6.4	+3.6
1983	Purchases	−16.7	−19.1	−35.8	−20.4
	Sales	+8.3	+12.9	+21.2	+12.6
	Balance	−8.4	−6.2	−14.5	−7.8
1984	Purchases	—	−28.9	−28.9	−3.0
	Sales	+4.7	+7.6	+12.3	+4.4
	Balance	+4.7	−21.4	−16.6	+1.4
1985	Purchases	—	−29.1	−29.1	−0.2
	Sales	+0.4	+30.8	+31.1	—
	Balance	+0.4	+1.6	+2.0	−0.2
1986	Purchases	−19.0	−33.6	−52.6	−12.2
	Sales	+4.1	+74.0	+78.1	+3.8
	Balance	−14.8	+40.4	+25.5	−8.4
1987	Purchases	—	−47.8	−47.8	−7.3
	Sales	+15.0	+61.7	+76.8	+25.4
	Balance	+15.0	+13.9	+28.9	+18.1
1988	Purchases	—	−26.8	−26.8	−6.1
	Sales	—	+16.3	+16.3	—
	Balance	—	−10.5	−10.5	−6.1
1989	Purchases	—	−20.4	−20.4	−3.0
	Sales	+5.0	+8.6	+13.6	+3.0
	Balance	+5.0	−11.8	−6.8	0.0

Source: Deutsche Bundesbank, *Annual Report*, 1989.

Note: Deutsche mark intervention by other central banks participating in the EMS exchange rate mechanism and EMS interventions by the Bundesbank. Plus (+) equals deutsche mark sales or expansionary impact on liquidity in Germany. Minus (−) equals deutsche mark purchases or contractionary impact on liquidity in Germany.

[1]Indicates the extent to which deutsche mark interventions in the EMS and the settlement of creditor and debtor positions in the EMCF affected the net external position of the Bundesbank and thus the banks' provision with central bank money; excludes transactions connected with the winding-up of the snake, which was succeeded by the EMS.

[2]As of the beginning of the EMS on March 13, 1979.

Table 7. Composition of the ECU

	National Currency Units		Percentage Weights		
	September 17, 1984	September 21, 1989	September 17, 1984	September 21, 1989	Change in percent
Deutsche mark	0.719	0.624	32.0	30.10	−5.9
French franc	1.31	1.33	19.0	19.00	—
Pound sterling	0.0878	0.0878	15.0	13.00	−13.3
Italian lira	140.0	152.0	10.2	10.15	−0.5
Netherlands guilder	0.256	0.220	10.1	9.40	−6.9
Belgian franc	3.71	3.30	8.2	7.60	−7.3
Luxembourg franc	0.14	0.13	0.3	0.30	—
Danish krone	0.219	0.198	2.7	2.45	−9.3
Irish pound	0.00871	0.00855	1.2	1.10	−8.3
Greek drachma	1.15	1.44	1.3	0.80	−38.5
Spanish peseta	—	6.89	—	5.30	. . .
Portuguese escudo	—	1.39	—	0.80	. . .

Source: European Community documents.

Table 8. Percentage Weights of Member Currencies in the ECU[1]

(Annual second quarter average)

	1975[2]	1979	1980	1981	1982	1983	1984	1985	1986	1987	1988	1989[3]
Belgian franc	8.0	9.1	9.1	8.8	8.1	8.1	8.0	8.2	8.4	8.6	8.5	7.6
Danish krone	3.0	3.0	2.8	2.7	2.7	2.7	2.6	2.7	2.7	2.8	2.8	2.4
French franc	21.7	19.7	19.7	19.1	18.3	16.9	16.7	19.2	19.1	18.9	18.6	19.0
Deutsche mark	26.9	32.8	32.9	32.7	34.7	36.5	37.0	32.0	33.4	34.6	34.6	30.1
Irish pound	1.4	1.1	1.1	1.1	1.1	1.1	1.0	1.2	1.2	1.1	1.1	1.1
Italian lira	13.3	9.7	9.2	8.6	8.2	8.1	7.9	9.8	9.5	9.4	9.1	10.1
Luxembourg franc	0.3	0.3	0.3	0.3	0.3	0.3	0.3	0.3	0.3	0.3	0.3	0.3
Netherlands guilder	9.1	10.4	10.3	10.2	10.8	11.2	11.4	10.1	10.6	10.9	11.0	9.4
Sterling	16.1	13.8	14.5	16.5	15.7	15.1	14.8	15.1	13.7	12.5	13.3	13.0
Greek drachma	—	—	—	—	—	—	—	1.2	0.9	0.8	0.7	0.8
Spanish peseta	—	—	—	—	—	—	—	—	—	—	—	5.3
Portuguese escudo	—	—	—	—	—	—	—	—	—	—	—	0.8
Total	100.0	100.0	100.0	100.0	100.0	100.0	100.0	100.0	100.0	100.0	100.0	100.0

Memorandum

Value of 1 ECU in terms of:

	1975[2]	1979	1980	1981	1982	1983	1984	1985	1986	1987	1988	1989[3]
Belgian franc	45.53	40.34	40.36	41.43	45.10	45.23	45.61	45.12	43.93	43.04	43.44	43.50
Danish krone	7.16	7.15	7.83	7.97	8.13	8.08	8.21	8.05	7.96	7.82	7.94	8.09
French franc	5.29	5.83	5.85	6.03	6.29	6.81	6.87	6.83	6.85	6.93	7.03	7.04
Deutsche mark	3.08	2.52	2.51	2.54	2.38	2.27	2.24	2.25	2.15	2.08	2.08	2.08
Irish pound	0.55	0.66	0.67	0.69	0.69	0.72	0.73	0.72	0.71	0.78	0.78	0.78
Italian lira	819.45	1128.65	1182.76	1263.36	1321.97	1346.57	1382.75	1429.76	1494.78	1494.41	1543.25	1513.68
Luxembourg franc	45.53	40.34	40.36	41.43	45.10	45.23	45.61	45.12	43.93	43.04	43.44	43.50
Netherlands guilder	3.14	2.75	2.76	2.81	2.64	2.55	2.52	2.53	2.42	2.34	2.33	2.34
Sterling	0.55	0.64	0.61	0.54	0.56	0.59	0.59	0.58	0.64	0.70	0.66	0.66
Greek drachma	—	—	—	—	—	—	—	98.54	134.97	154.36	166.40	177.39
Spanish peseta	—	—	—	—	—	—	—	—	—	—	—	130.79
Portuguese escudo	—	—	—	—	—	—	—	—	—	—	—	172.24
U.S. dollar	1.29	1.33	1.39	1.12	1.00	0.91	0.83	0.73	0.96	1.15	1.22	1.08
Japanese yen	292.40	290.06	322.39	245.41	244.66	216.65	189.48	182.17	163.15	164.09	152.96	148.47
Swiss franc	2.57	2.28	2.34	2.27	2.00	1.89	1.85	1.88	1.79	1.72	1.73	1.82

Sources: International Monetary Fund, *International Financial Statistics*, Data Fund, and Fund staff calculations.

[1]Calculations of percentage weights are based on New York noon quotations. The weights may not add because of rounding.

[2]Weights are those of the European Unit of Account (EUA), which was introduced in certain areas of EC activities as of April 21, 1975. The EUA is defined as a basket of all ECU currencies; this basket was also used for defining the ECU in 1979.

[3]Using currency composition of ECU effective September 21, 1989.

Table 9. Creation of ECUs by Swap Operations, 1979–89

Swap Operations Starting In		Gold Transfers (Million ounces)	U.S. Dollar Transfers (Billions)	Gold Price (ECUs per ounce)	US$1 per ECU	Counterpart in ECUs (Billions)		
						Gold	U.S. dollars	Total
1979	II	80.7	13.4	165	1.34	13.3	10.0	23.3
1979	III	85.3	15.9	185	1.37	15.8	11.6	27.4
1979	IV	85.3	16.0	211	1.42	18.0	11.3	29.3
1980	I	85.5	15.5	259	1.45	22.2	10.7	32.9
1980	II	85.6	14.4	370	1.30	31.7	11.1	42.8
1980	III	85.6	13.7	419	1.43	35.9	9.6	45.5
1980	IV	85.6	13.9	425	1.40	36.4	9.9	46.3
1981	I	85.6	14.5	447	1.33	38.3	10.9	49.2
1981	II	85.7	14.2	440	1.10	37.7	12.0	49.7
1981	III	85.7	12.7	406	1.03	34.8	12.3	47.1
1981	IV	85.7	11.5	402	1.10	34.5	10.5	45.0
1982	I	85.7	11.7	368	1.09	31.6	10.7	42.3
1982	II	85.7	10.5	327	1.00	28.0	10.5	38.6
1982	III	85.7	9.9	324	0.96	27.8	10.3	38.1
1982	IV	85.7	10.0	367	0.93	31.5	10.8	42.3
1983	I	85.7	10.0	429	0.98	36.7	10.2	47.0
1983	II	85.7	10.5	452	0.94	38.8	11.2	50.0
1983	III	85.7	10.5	465	0.89	39.9	11.8	51.7
1983	IV	85.7	10.6	477	0.87	40.9	12.2	53.1
1984	I	85.7	10.6	461	0.81	39.5	13.1	52.6
1984	II	85.7	10.8	452	0.85	38.7	12.7	51.4
1984	III	85.7	10.6	460	0.80	39.5	13.3	52.8
1984	IV	85.7	10.1	454	0.74	39.0	13.6	52.6
1985	I	85.7	10.2	434	0.70	37.2	14.5	51.7
1985	II	85.7	9.0	449	0.71	38.5	12.6	51.1
1985	III	85.7	10.0	429	0.74	36.8	13.5	50.3
1985	IV	86.5	10.5	396	0.84	34.0	12.5	46.5
1986	I	86.5	10.6	368	0.88	31.8	12.0	43.8
1986	II	86.5	11.2	373	0.91	32.3	12.3	44.6
1986	III	86.5	12.3	355	0.99	30.7	12.4	43.1
1986	IV	86.5	14.3	366	1.04	31.7	13.7	45.4
1987	I	86.5	14.2	365	1.08	31.6	13.2	44.8
1987	II	86.5	16.3	368	1.14	31.9	14.3	46.1
1987	III	89.4	21.5	376	1.13	33.6	19.0	52.7
1987	IV	89.4	21.9	389	1.13	35.6	19.4	55.0
1988	I	93.4	24.9	376	1.28	35.1	19.5	54.6
1988	II	93.9	25.3	365	1.25	34.3	20.2	54.6
1988	III	93.9	24.4	369	1.14	34.7	21.5	56.2
1988	IV	94.0	22.6	361	1.11	34.0	20.3	54.3
1989	I	94.0	22.6	354	1.16	33.3	19.4	52.7
1989	II	93.6	22.2	348	1.11	32.6	20.0	52.6
1989	III	93.6	21.6	349	1.08	32.7	19.9	52.6
1989	IV	93.6	22.6	335	1.10	31.3	20.5	51.8

Source: Commission of the European Communities.

Table 10. Variability of Bilateral Nominal Exchange Rates, 1974–89[1]

	Coefficient of Variation						Variability of Log Changes					
	1974–78	1979–89	1986	1987	1988	1989	1974–78	1979–89	1986	1987	1988	1989
	Against ERM Currencies											
Belgium	20.3	10.6	10.9	4.9	2.7	3.1	10.6	6.0	6.0	3.3	2.1	3.1
Denmark	25.0	12.3	11.2	9.5	5.0	5.1	12.8	6.7	5.8	6.2	4.1	4.5
France	31.6	13.8	23.6	6.9	4.8	5.0	16.8	6.8	8.8	4.5	3.3	4.5
Germany, Fed. Rep. of	29.2	13.2	14.2	7.6	3.9	4.8	14.7	6.0	5.1	4.5	2.8	4.3
Ireland	36.0	12.9	41.4	5.3	5.2	5.0	18.4	7.9	28.4	3.9	2.9	4.1
Italy	36.0	15.5	11.5	10.9	4.9	8.9	19.3	7.5	4.3	5.6	4.0	7.6
Netherlands	21.1	10.6	10.1	6.5	3.6	3.5	11.1	5.2	4.2	3.5	3.1	3.1
Average ERM[2]	28.4	12.7	17.6	7.4	4.3	5.1	14.8	6.6	8.9	4.5	3.2	4.4
Austria	20.3	9.6	8.4	4.9	2.7	3.2	9.9	4.3	3.4	3.2	2.2	2.8
Canada	44.1	49.1	54.2	31.2	62.6	27.8	22.5	24.9	21.1	25.9	30.6	25.6
Japan	44.5	44.4	39.9	25.3	33.8	52.1	21.1	20.4	24.5	20.3	10.5	16.8
Norway	25.3	26.6	65.1	23.0	17.9	17.8	13.3	12.8	16.3	14.4	11.1	8.5
Sweden	30.2	27.2	29.5	12.9	17.4	17.8	14.6	14.3	9.4	9.1	6.9	11.1
Switzerland	44.0	22.5	24.4	14.4	10.4	17.3	20.5	12.0	11.9	9.3	5.3	13.5
United Kingdom	32.7	38.9	64.0	26.8	25.4	47.0	16.8	19.7	26.4	14.3	14.7	14.3
United States	34.7	51.3	58.7	35.2	47.2	32.9	18.8	26.4	20.0	22.7	26.8	29.0
Average non-ERM[2]	34.5	33.7	43.0	21.7	27.2	27.0	17.2	16.8	16.6	14.9	13.5	15.2
Average European non-ERM[2]	30.5	25.0	38.3	16.4	14.8	20.6	15.0	12.6	13.5	10.1	8.0	10.0
	Against Non-ERM Currencies											
Belgium	36.7	43.8	48.6	28.7	35.8	35.2	17.9	21.9	17.0	19.4	18.7	22.0
Denmark	32.3	41.5	49.2	29.4	35.6	36.1	17.0	21.6	17.6	20.2	18.0	22.4
France	37.8	46.5	44.3	28.5	38.4	36.0	18.7	22.5	22.9	18.6	18.7	21.6
Germany, Fed. Rep. of	35.7	40.1	50.1	27.9	32.8	35.8	18.0	20.7	18.0	18.6	16.9	20.9
Ireland	37.0	43.3	37.5	31.3	36.2	35.2	14.4	22.9	27.5	19.3	20.6	22.3
Italy	38.0	44.3	50.0	30.0	38.1	33.4	20.1	20.0	19.5	18.1	18.5	18.3
Netherlands	36.8	43.8	55.5	31.9	39.6	36.1	18.4	22.5	18.5	20.7	20.8	23.0
Average ERM[2]	36.3	43.3	47.9	29.7	36.7	35.4	17.8	21.7	20.1	19.3	18.9	21.5
Austria	39.5	44.6	54.8	31.1	38.1	38.1	18.6	23.1	19.5	20.9	19.6	23.2
Canada	23.4	19.0	15.7	16.5	24.9	15.6	12.4	12.1	9.4	13.2	14.6	8.4
Japan	46.7	52.0	74.9	48.4	29.2	46.7	20.1	27.2	34.0	30.7	24.3	20.0
Norway	35.6	36.9	41.0	27.6	30.0	26.2	18.7	18.9	24.2	16.3	18.5	15.6
Sweden	39.9	38.0	37.0	25.3	25.8	23.0	18.6	18.2	16.0	16.1	16.6	14.1
Switzerland	48.0	46.2	56.6	34.6	47.7	33.4	23.6	24.5	21.1	22.8	21.3	24.6
United Kingdom	49.6	46.4	45.4	37.3	28.6	34.2	18.9	23.5	22.7	21.9	23.9	19.4
United States	34.2	37.1	44.1	34.9	29.0	30.7	16.0	20.3	20.3	21.6	21.1	16.6
Average non-ERM[2]	39.6	40.0	46.2	32.0	31.6	31.0	18.4	21.0	20.9	20.5	20.0	17.7
Average European non-ERM[2]	42.5	42.4	47.0	31.2	34.0	31.0	19.7	21.6	20.7	19.6	20.0	19.4

Source: International Monetary Fund, *International Financial Statistics*, various issues.

[1]Weighted average (multilateral exchange rate model (MERM) weights) of variability of bilateral exchange rates against ERM or non-ERM currencies, with variability measured by coefficient of variation or standard deviation of log changes of average monthly bilateral exchange rates.

[2]Unweighted average.

Table 11. Variability of Bilateral Real Exchange Rates, 1974–89[1]

| | Against ERM Currencies | | | | | | | | | | | | Against Non-ERM Currencies | | | | | | | | | | | |
| | Coefficient of variation | | | | | | Variability of log changes | | | | | | Coefficient of variation | | | | | | Variability of log changes | | | | | |
	1974–78	1979–89	1986	1987	1988	1989	1974–78	1979–89	1986	1987	1988	1989	1974–78	1979–89	1986	1987	1988	1989	1974–78	1979–89	1986	1987	1988	1989
Belgium	21.9	11.3	8.7	4.8	3.9	4.8	11.9	6.9	7.0	4.2	2.7	3.5	35.8	43.4	45.2	26.9	40.7	34.6	18.7	22.8	18.1	20.0	18.6	22.8
Denmark	25.8	12.5	15.5	9.1	7.6	7.7	16.9	8.8	11.8	8.3	5.8	5.1	37.3	41.5	53.7	29.1	38.4	36.2	20.3	22.7	18.2	21.3	20.0	22.3
France	30.4	14.7	18.5	5.5	6.6	6.7	17.3	7.5	8.6	5.0	4.0	4.6	35.3	44.1	43.1	27.5	41.1	35.3	19.0	23.4	23.1	19.7	19.1	22.5
Germany, Fed. Rep. of	28.0	13.2	10.7	5.8	6.0	8.4	15.8	6.8	6.0	5.5	3.3	5.0	32.8	41.5	43.6	28.3	40.1	34.0	19.3	21.7	18.6	20.4	17.9	22.3
Ireland	27.7	16.7	45.5	7.1	7.6	13.9	20.0	11.1	28.6	4.6	7.9	7.5	33.4	41.1	33.7	31.1	44.2	27.5	19.0	22.8	29.6	20.2	23.2	20.0
Italy	26.1	15.9	14.4	6.3	10.3	11.5	20.0	8.1	5.0	6.1	4.9	7.3	32.3	40.9	52.2	29.6	39.1	36.3	20.8	21.3	20.7	19.8	20.2	19.4
Netherlands	21.1	11.1	9.6	5.1	5.6	5.5	13.0	6.3	6.3	4.4	4.4	3.6	34.3	45.2	50.7	30.2	45.7	34.7	19.9	23.6	19.9	21.6	21.6	23.6
Average ERM[2]	25.9	13.6	17.5	6.2	6.8	8.4	16.4	7.9	10.5	5.4	4.7	5.2	34.5	42.5	46.0	29.0	41.3	34.1	19.6	22.6	21.2	20.4	20.1	21.9
Austria	19.3	9.9	9.1	7.2	6.5	7.0	11.7	6.5	4.7	5.6	5.5	6.1	35.5	45.1	50.9	28.3	42.1	35.6	19.9	24.4	21.0	21.3	18.6	25.4
Canada	43.3	49.1	46.2	30.1	66.8	31.2	23.4	25.3	20.2	26.3	31.4	26.5	21.9	20.6	20.5	15.9	24.6	17.6	13.6	13.1	11.5	13.5	15.0	8.7
Japan	40.9	42.4	39.6	27.8	32.2	51.4	22.4	21.4	25.9	24.2	10.8	18.8	44.0	53.9	70.1	44.8	30.8	48.6	22.4	29.0	35.9	33.6	25.7	20.6
Norway	24.7	26.1	42.2	28.4	23.0	18.3	14.5	13.7	18.7	15.6	11.8	10.2	31.7	36.3	35.7	29.6	31.6	25.5	19.1	20.3	26.3	18.0	20.1	16.1
Sweden	28.1	28.6	26.5	11.9	25.4	14.8	16.2	15.6	10.4	9.5	8.3	11.9	34.2	37.3	33.9	25.8	25.1	24.9	20.1	19.1	17.0	17.5	17.5	14.6
Switzerland	35.7	21.0	20.4	12.3	15.1	16.1	21.5	11.9	11.1	9.4	5.3	13.3	43.5	47.1	52.2	33.6	55.0	37.2	24.7	25.2	21.8	24.8	22.3	26.4
United Kingdom	28.4	41.9	58.1	30.8	38.4	35.4	17.5	21.8	27.9	14.9	17.0	14.5	40.1	47.6	43.8	37.9	29.8	31.7	20.8	26.0	25.1	23.4	25.5	19.8
United States	33.0	50.1	57.7	32.5	52.6	33.8	19.7	27.2	20.5	23.5	27.7	29.4	31.6	38.8	45.9	32.9	30.2	31.4	17.6	21.6	22.5	23.0	22.1	16.8
Average non-ERM[2]	31.7	33.6	37.4	22.6	32.5	26.0	18.4	17.9	17.4	16.1	14.7	16.3	35.3	40.8	44.1	31.1	33.7	31.6	19.8	22.3	22.6	21.9	20.9	18.6
Average European non-ERM[2]	27.2	25.5	31.2	18.1	21.7	18.3	16.3	13.9	14.6	11.0	9.6	11.2	37.0	42.7	43.3	31.0	36.7	31.0	20.9	23.0	22.2	21.0	20.8	20.5

Source: International Monetary Fund, *International Financial Statistics*, various issues.
[1] Weighted average (multilateral exchange rate model (MERM) weights) of variability of bilateral real exchange rates (nominal exchange rates adjusted for relative consumer price movements—wholesale prices for Ireland) against ERM or non-ERM currencies, with variability measured by coefficient of variation or standard deviation of log changes of average monthly bilateral exchange rates.
[2] Unweighted average.

Table 12. Variability of Nominal and Real Effective Exchange Rates, 1975–89

	Nominal Effective Rate[1]						Real Effective Rate[2]					
	1975–78	1979–89	1986	1987	1988	1989	1975–78	1979–89	1986	1987	1988	1989
Belgium	18.9	15.0	14.4	6.5	12.4	11.1	28.1	25.1	12.5	27.3	13.4	18.1
Denmark	18.9	21.5	25.7	13.7	21.9	20.4	32.9	24.9	36.8	13.5	33.0	19.2
France	21.2	22.9	13.0	6.3	19.4	15.5	28.5	19.5	26.7	19.4	10.7	15.8
Germany, Fed. Rep. of	25.2	20.4	29.0	11.8	16.2	18.2	27.7	20.3	44.0	14.8	20.3	8.3
Ireland	34.7	20.1	19.1	11.4	18.8	14.7	21.7	22.2	26.8	11.9	32.9	15.3
Italy	25.9	19.9	20.8	11.7	19.2	12.2	25.0	15.7	30.6	10.6	10.6	13.7
Netherlands	19.5	18.4	27.7	12.7	18.4	13.9	19.2	22.8	44.1	9.4	9.8	2.3
Average ERM[3]	23.5	19.8	21.4	10.6	18.0	15.1	26.2	21.5	31.6	15.3	18.7	13.2
Austria	21.1	22.7	30.7	13.0	21.3	18.9	17.1	17.5	21.7	24.7	21.2	15.2
Canada	26.0	16.5	11.9	11.3	27.8	13.3	23.5	20.3	13.2	9.6	31.9	22.1
Japan	42.7	41.1	60.4	37.6	19.4	45.2	35.8	42.0	57.7	23.1	13.6	40.5
Norway	25.1	18.2	41.9	14.4	16.4	4.4	23.5	23.2	25.5	13.0	39.5	35.9
Sweden	26.7	15.8	2.1	5.1	7.3	2.3	59.8	31.8	20.2	10.4	32.7	39.4
Switzerland	57.2	27.9	39.8	21.4	31.4	16.2	45.2	23.2	17.1	25.2	30.9	12.7
United Kingdom	67.3	34.9	46.3	28.7	16.7	36.1	42.2	43.6	66.7	31.3	18.5	24.3
United States	21.8	35.2	41.7	32.5	26.2	24.7	24.3	38.1	52.1	31.7	30.4	21.1
Average non-ERM[3]	36.0	26.5	34.4	20.5	20.8	20.1	33.9	30.0	34.3	21.1	27.3	26.4
Average European non-ERM[3]	39.5	23.9	32.2	16.5	18.6	15.6	37.5	27.9	30.2	20.9	28.6	25.5

Source: International Monetary Fund, *International Financial Statistics*, various issues.

[1]Based on the multilateral exchange rate model (MERM) and monthly data. Variability is measured by the coefficient of variation (multiplied by 1,000) of average monthly effective exchange rates.

[2]Trade-weighted exchange rates adjusted for relative unit labor cost changes. Variability is measured by the coefficient of variation (multiplied by 1,000) of average quarterly effective exchange rates.

[3]Unweighted average.

Table 13. External Current Account, 1975–89

(In percent of GDP/GNP)

	1975–78	1979–82	1983–86	1987	1988	1989[1]
Belgium	−0.2	−3.5	0.7	2.1	2.3	2.1
Denmark	−3.1	−3.9	−3.9	−3.0	−1.7	−1.9
France	0.3	−0.7	−0.2	−0.5	−0.4	−0.6
Germany, Fed. Rep. of	1.0	−0.5	2.3	4.0	4.0	4.5
Ireland	−4.7	−12.6	−5.2	1.5	4.1	3.3
Italy	0.4	−1.1	−0.2	−0.2	−0.6	−0.9
Netherlands	1.6	1.3	3.7	1.6	2.4	2.3
Average ERM	−0.7	−3.0	−0.4	0.8	1.4	1.2
Standard deviation	2.1	4.2	3.0	2.1	2.2	2.2
Difference between highest and lowest value	6.3	13.9	8.8	7.0	5.8	6.4
Coefficient of variation[2]	321.6	141.4	766.6	263.1	152.1	179.3
Austria	−2.2	−1.2	0.0	−0.2	−0.4	−0.6
Norway	−7.8	1.2	1.9	−4.9	−4.0	1.5
Spain	−2.0	−1.8	0.8	0.1	−1.1	−2.7
Sweden	−1.4	−3.0	−0.5	−0.5	−1.4	−1.6
Switzerland	5.4	2.3	4.6	4.1	3.3	3.6
United Kingdom	−0.4	1.4	0.7	−0.9	−3.2	−3.7
Average other Europe	−1.4	−0.2	1.3	−0.4	−1.1	−0.6
Standard deviation	3.8	1.9	1.7	2.6	2.3	2.5
Difference between highest and lowest value	13.1	5.3	5.1	9.0	7.3	7.3
Coefficient of variation[2]	274.8	961.2	132.7	666.2	204.5	410.5
Australia	−2.7	−3.5	−4.9	−4.2	−4.4	−5.7
Canada	−2.2	−0.8	−0.3	−1.7	−1.7	−2.9
Japan	0.9	−0.2	3.1	3.6	2.8	2.5
United States	−0.0	0.0	−2.5	−3.2	−2.6	−2.4
Average other industrial	−1.0	−1.1	−1.1	−1.4	−1.5	−2.1
Standard deviation	1.5	1.4	2.9	3.0	2.6	3.0
Difference between highest and lowest value	3.6	3.6	8.0	7.8	7.2	8.2
Coefficient of variation[2]	152.4	126.3	261.4	222.0	178.1	139.0
Average non-ERM	−1.2	−0.6	0.3	−0.8	−1.3	−1.2
Standard deviation	3.1	1.8	2.5	2.8	2.5	2.8
Difference between highest and lowest value	13.1	5.8	9.4	9.0	7.7	9.3
Coefficient of variation[2]	253.6	314.2	844.1	362.1	193.1	229.3

Source: International Monetary Fund, *World Economic Outlook,* October 1990.
[1]Preliminary.
[2]Absolute value of standard deviation divided by mean and multiplied by 100.

Table 14. External Trade Account, 1975–89

(In percent of GDP/GNP)

	1975–78	1979–82	1983–86	1987	1988	1989[1]
Belgium	−1.4	−3.1	0.7	1.7	1.9	1.7
Denmark	−5.1	−2.8	−0.6	0.8	1.7	2.0
France	−0.5	−1.8	−1.0	−1.0	−0.9	−1.1
Germany, Fed. Rep. of	3.9	2.5	4.5	6.3	6.5	6.9
Ireland	−7.5	−11.5	2.4	9.8	13.8	14.1
Italy	−0.4	−2.3	−0.7	−0.0	−0.1	−0.6
Netherlands	0.3	1.1	4.0	2.5	2.9	2.8
Average ERM	−1.5	−2.6	1.3	2.9	3.7	3.7
Standard deviation	3.5	4.1	2.1	3.6	4.7	4.9
Difference between highest and lowest value	11.4	14.0	5.5	10.8	14.7	15.2
Coefficient of variation[2]	225.2	161.8	160.6	124.2	126.6	132.1
Austria	−6.7	−7.0	−5.3	−4.4	−4.5	−5.0
Norway	−6.6	2.9	5.3	−1.1	−0.4	5.6
Spain	−5.4	−4.9	−3.3	−4.5	−5.2	−6.7
Sweden	−0.5	−1.2	2.5	2.4	2.3	2.4
Switzerland	0.5	−3.1	−3.0	−2.6	−2.7	−3.2
United Kingdom	−2.2	0.2	−1.2	−2.6	−4.6	−4.9
Average other Europe	−3.5	−2.2	−0.8	−2.1	−2.5	−1.9
Standard deviation	2.9	3.3	3.6	2.3	2.7	4.4
Difference between highest and lowest value	7.2	9.9	10.6	6.9	7.5	12.3
Coefficient of variation[2]	83.1	151.7	432.5	108.7	106.5	229.2
Australia	1.5	0.2	−0.2	−0.3	−0.4	−0.9
Canada	0.9	2.8	3.5	2.1	1.6	0.9
Japan	1.9	0.9	3.8	4.0	3.3	3.2
United States	−0.8	−1.0	−2.9	−3.5	−2.6	−2.2
Average other industrial countries	0.9	0.7	1.1	0.6	0.5	0.2
Standard deviation	1.0	1.4	2.8	2.8	2.2	2.0
Difference between highest and lowest value	2.7	3.8	6.6	7.5	5.9	5.4
Coefficient of variation[2]	113.4	191.6	261.8	495.5	453.0	805.2
Average non-ERM	−1.7	−1.0	−0.1	−1.1	−1.3	−1.1
Standard deviation	3.2	3.0	3.4	2.9	2.9	3.8
Difference between highest and lowest value	8.7	9.9	10.6	8.5	8.5	12.3
Coefficient of variation[2]	183.5	301.7	4,197.1	269.9	221.2	359.4

Source: International Monetary Fund, *World Economic Outlook*, October 1990.

[1] Preliminary.

[2] Absolute value of standard deviation divided by mean and multiplied by 100.

Table 15. External Current Account, 1975–89

(In billions of U.S. dollars)

	1975–78	1979–82	1983–86	1987	1988	1989
Belgium	−0.2	−3.7	0.8	2.8	3.4	3.8
Denmark	−1.4	−2.4	−2.6	−3.0	−1.8	−1.5
France	0.8	−4.1	−0.7	−4.4	−3.6	−3.3
Germany, Fed. Rep. of	5.2	−4.4	17.8	45.2	48.6	52.8
Ireland	−0.4	−1.4	−0.6	0.5	0.5	0.6
Italy	1.3	−4.9	−0.5	−1.5	−5.2	−10.9
Netherlands	0.7	1.0	4.8	3.2	4.6	6.1
Total ERM	6.1	−20.0	19.0	42.8	46.5	47.6
Austria	−1.0	−0.8	−0.8	−0.2	−0.3	0.1
Norway	−3.3	0.7	0.9	−4.1	−3.7	1.7
Spain	−2.1	−3.5	1.6	0.3	−3.6	−10.8
Sweden	−1.1	−3.4	−0.5	−0.9	−2.3	−3.7
Switzerland	2.8	0.9	5.1	7.6	8.4	5.9
United Kingdom	−0.9	6.7	3.1	−6.1	−26.3	−34.2
Total other Europe	−5.6	0.6	9.3	−3.5	−27.7	−41.0
Australia	−2.7	−5.6	−8.0	−8.2	−10.9	−16.6
Canada	−4.3	−2.0	−1.1	−7.1	−8.4	−16.6
Japan	7.6	−2.0	47.7	87.0	79.6	57.2
United States	−1.9	0.4	−98.6	−143.7	−126.5	−106.0
Total other industrial countries	−1.2	−9.1	−60.1	−71.9	−66.2	−82.1
Total non-ERM	−6.8	−8.5	−50.7	−75.4	−93.9	−123.1

Source: International Monetary Fund, *World Economic Outlook*, October 1990.

Table 16.   External Trade Balances of ERM Countries, 1975–89

(In billions of U.S. dollars)

	1975–78	1979–82	1983–86	1987	1988	1989
Against ERM partners						
Belgium	−0.0	0.2	−1.0	0.1	−1.7	−0.1
Denmark	−1.7	−1.3	−1.6	−2.0	−1.5	−1.0
France	−2.9	−6.4	−7.4	−12.3	−12.2	−13.7
Germany, Fed. Rep. of	2.2	5.5	6.9	20.2	26.3	28.5
Ireland	0.1	0.3	1.2	2.9	3.3	3.9
Italy	−0.5	−4.5	−5.0	−10.3	−13.5	−16.1
Netherlands	4.3	10.8	11.7	7.4	8.2	9.2
Against rest of world						
Belgium	−2.7	−6.1	−1.2	−0.4	1.6	1.7
Denmark	−1.0	−0.9	0.7	2.2	2.8	2.4
France	−1.1	−8.3	0.2	2.2	−1.3	0.4
Germany, Fed. Rep. of	14.4	7.1	21.3	45.6	46.6	43.2
Ireland	−1.1	−2.8	−1.1	−0.6	−0.1	−0.6
Italy	−2.7	−9.5	−3.1	1.6	3.5	4.2
Netherlands	−6.2	−11.9	−8.0	−6.0	−4.5	−5.9
Total ERM	1.0	−27.8	13.5	50.6	57.5	56.0

Source: International Monetary Fund, *Direction of Trade Statistics*.

Table 17. Consumer Price Indices, 1975–89

(Annual change in percent)

	1975–78	1979–82	1983–86	1987	1988	1989
Belgium	8.4	6.9	5.0	1.6	1.2	3.1
Denmark	9.9	10.9	5.4	4.0	4.9	4.8
France	10.0	12.3	6.3	3.3	2.7	3.5
Germany, Fed. Rep. of	4.2	5.3	1.9	0.2	1.3	2.8
Ireland	14.2	17.3	7.1	3.2	2.1	4.0
Italy	16.1	18.0	9.7	4.7	5.0	6.3
Netherlands	7.5	5.8	2.1	−0.8	0.7	1.1
Average ERM	10.0	10.9	5.4	2.3	2.6	3.6
Standard deviation	3.7	4.9	2.5	1.9	1.6	1.5
Difference between highest and lowest value	11.9	12.7	7.8	5.5	4.2	5.2
Coefficient of variation[1]	37.3	44.6	47.4	80.9	63.6	41.8
Austria	6.2	5.6	3.5	1.4	1.9	2.7
Norway	9.5	10.2	3.1	8.7	6.7	4.6
Spain	19.0	15.1	10.3	5.2	4.8	6.8
Sweden	11.0	10.3	7.1	4.2	5.8	8.9
Switzerland	2.7	4.9	2.5	1.4	1.9	3.5
United Kingdom	17.8	13.0	4.8	4.1	4.9	7.9
Average other Europe	11.0	9.8	5.2	4.2	4.3	5.7
Standard deviation	5.8	3.6	2.7	2.5	1.8	2.3
Difference between highest and lowest value	16.3	10.1	7.7	7.3	4.8	6.3
Coefficient of variation[1]	52.9	37.1	51.9	59.2	42.2	40.1
Australia	12.2	9.7	8.4	9.3	7.3	7.3
Canada	8.8	10.6	4.6	4.4	4.0	5.0
Japan	8.4	4.8	1.7	0.1	0.7	2.3
United States	7.3	10.3	3.3	3.6	4.1	4.8
Average other industrial countries	9.2	8.9	4.5	4.4	4.0	4.8
Standard deviation	1.8	2.4	2.5	3.3	2.3	1.8
Difference between highest and lowest value	4.9	5.9	6.7	9.2	6.6	5.0
Coefficient of variation[1]	20.1	26.8	55.4	75.3	58.0	36.6
Average non-ERM	10.3	9.4	4.9	4.2	4.2	5.4
Standard deviation	4.8	3.2	2.6	2.8	2.1	2.2
Difference between highest and lowest value	16.3	10.3	8.6	9.2	6.6	6.6
Coefficient of variation[1]	46.3	34.2	53.7	66.5	48.7	40.0

Source: International Monetary Fund, *World Economic Outlook*, October 1990.
[1]Absolute value of standard deviation divided by mean and multiplied by 100.

Table 18.   GNP Deflators, 1975–89

(Annual change in percent)

	1975–78	1979–82	1983–86	1987	1988	1989
Belgium	8.0	5.1	5.4	1.8	0.9	2.6
Denmark	10.2	9.1	5.6	5.0	4.9	4.6
France	10.9	11.1	7.0	2.9	3.1	2.7
Germany, Fed. Rep. of	4.4	4.3	2.6	2.0	1.4	2.5
Ireland	16.5	15.4	7.0	2.0	2.9	4.0
Italy	16.9	17.7	10.7	6.1	6.2	6.3
Netherlands	7.8	5.2	1.5	−0.5	1.8	2.7
Average ERM	10.7	9.7	5.7	2.6	3.1	3.6
Standard deviation	4.3	4.9	2.8	2.1	1.8	1.3
Difference between highest and lowest value	12.5	13.4	9.3	6.6	5.3	3.9
Coefficient of variation[1]	40.0	50.7	49.8	80.6	58.2	36.8
Austria	5.7	5.5	3.9	2.4	2.0	2.6
Norway	8.1	11.3	4.0	6.0	4.4	5.6
Spain	19.1	14.1	10.5	5.9	5.7	6.8
Sweden	11.3	9.5	7.7	4.8	6.6	7.3
Switzerland	3.4	4.7	3.2	2.6	2.2	3.5
United Kingdom	16.9	13.2	4.8	4.9	6.6	6.7
Average other Europe	10.7	9.7	5.7	4.4	4.6	5.4
Standard deviation	5.7	3.6	2.6	1.4	1.9	1.8
Difference between highest and lowest value	15.6	9.4	7.4	3.6	4.6	4.7
Coefficient of variation[1]	52.8	36.8	45.8	32.5	41.2	32.6
Australia	11.7	10.1	7.5	7.4	9.0	7.9
Canada	7.7	10.0	3.3	4.3	4.1	4.9
Japan	6.4	3.0	1.3	−0.3	0.6	1.5
United States	7.5	8.5	3.3	3.1	3.3	4.2
Average other industrial countries	8.3	7.9	3.8	3.6	4.2	4.6
Standard deviation	2.0	2.9	2.2	2.8	3.0	2.3
Difference between highest and lowest value	5.4	7.2	6.2	7.7	8.4	6.4
Coefficient of variation[1]	24.2	37.0	58.6	76.1	71.9	49.0
Average non-ERM	9.8	9.0	4.9	4.1	4.4	5.1
Standard deviation	4.7	3.5	2.6	2.1	2.4	2.0
Difference between highest and lowest value	15.6	11.1	9.2	7.7	8.4	6.4
Coefficient of variation[1]	48.3	38.3	53.1	51.4	54.5	39.6

Source: International Monetary Fund, *World Economic Outlook*, October 1990.
[1]Absolute value of standard deviation divided by mean and multiplied by 100.

Table 19.   Wages in Manufacturing, 1976–89

(Annual change in percent)

	1976–78	1979–82	1983–86	1987	1988	1989
Belgium	11.0	8.8	6.1	1.9	0.8	5.6
Denmark	10.8	10.3	5.7	11.1	1.8	3.2
France	13.6	16.0	8.0	3.1	4.0	4.5
Germany, Fed. Rep. of	8.5	6.9	5.0	4.6	4.2	4.3
Ireland	16.4	19.7	9.3	9.8	5.3	4.1
Italy	19.2	19.3	12.1	6.5	6.4	7.4
Netherlands	9.7	6.1	4.1	2.9	1.5	1.4
Average ERM	12.7	12.4	7.2	5.7	3.4	4.3
Standard deviation	3.6	5.4	2.6	3.3	1.9	1.7
Difference between highest and lowest value	10.8	13.7	8.0	9.1	5.6	6.0
Coefficient of variation[1]	28.3	43.2	36.0	58.1	56.8	40.0
Norway	13.3	9.7	9.6	16.1	1.5	3.8
Spain	31.7	19.8	9.5	9.9	7.0	7.0
Sweden	13.0	9.3	9.6	7.0	7.1	11.4
Switzerland	2.2	4.4	3.0	2.6	3.0	3.8
United Kingdom	15.1	16.0	7.2	6.8	9.0	9.6
Average other Europe	14.0	11.1	7.5	8.2	4.9	6.7
Standard deviation	9.0	5.2	2.4	4.1	2.9	2.9
Difference between highest and lowest value	29.5	15.4	6.6	13.5	7.5	7.7
Coefficient of variation[1]	63.9	47.0	32.6	50.7	58.9	43.4
Canada	10.9	11.6	5.1	5.2	6.2	5.4
Japan	7.3	6.4	3.9	2.3	3.4	6.5
United States	8.2	10.2	3.8	2.4	3.7	2.7
Average other industrial countries	8.8	9.4	4.2	3.3	4.4	4.9
Standard deviation	1.6	2.2	0.6	1.3	1.3	1.6
Difference between highest and lowest value	3.6	5.2	1.2	2.9	2.8	3.7
Coefficient of variation[1]	17.6	23.2	13.6	40.0	28.5	32.2
Average non-ERM	12.3	10.5	6.4	6.5	4.7	6.1
Standard deviation	7.8	4.5	2.5	4.2	2.5	2.7
Difference between highest and lowest value	29.5	15.4	6.6	13.8	7.5	8.7
Coefficient of variation[1]	63.3	42.8	39.5	63.5	52.3	44.1

Source: International Monetary Fund, *International Financial Statistics*.
[1]Absolute value of standard deviation divided by mean and multiplied by 100.

Table 20. Unit Labor Costs, 1976–88

(Annual change in percent)

	1976–78	1979–82	1983–86	1987	1988
Belgium	4.9	4.0	0.7	−3.3	−4.3
Denmark	5.4	6.0	3.1	9.3	0.3
France	8.9	12.0	3.8	−1.1	−1.1
Germany, Fed. Rep. of	4.9	4.1	1.6	1.4	1.0
Ireland	9.7	12.8	3.1	3.5	−0.7
Italy	14.8	15.5	8.0	3.0	3.0
Netherlands	4.9	2.3	0.3	−1.1	−2.2
Average ERM	7.6	8.1	2.9	1.7	−0.6
Standard deviation	3.5	4.9	2.4	3.8	2.2
Difference between highest and lowest value	9.9	13.3	7.7	12.6	7.3
Coefficient of variation[1]	45.4	60.0	81.5	228.0	370.7
Austria	3.3	2.6	1.2	2.3	−0.5
Norway	10.3	7.6	6.9	13.3	4.3
Spain	27.8	16.2	6.3	6.7	3.8
Sweden	9.7	7.0	7.0	4.6	4.7
Switzerland	−0.2	2.6	0.9	0.6	1.1
United Kingdom	11.9	13.4	4.6	4.2	6.1
Average other Europe	10.5	8.3	4.5	5.3	3.3
Standard deviation	8.8	5.1	2.5	4.0	2.3
Difference between highest and lowest value	28.0	13.7	6.1	12.7	6.6
Coefficient of variation[1]	84.3	61.9	56.7	76.4	69.8
Canada	8.6	9.9	2.6	3.0	4.0
Japan	2.6	2.2	−2.0	−2.9	−1.6
United States	6.1	8.3	1.6	0.5	1.5
Average other industrial countries	5.8	6.8	0.7	0.2	1.3
Standard deviation	2.5	3.3	2.0	2.4	2.3
Difference between highest and lowest value	6.0	7.7	4.6	5.9	5.6
Coefficient of variation[1]	42.7	48.8	268.4	1049.6	178.8
Average non-ERM	8.9	7.8	3.2	3.6	2.6
Standard deviation	7.7	4.6	3.0	4.3	2.5
Difference between highest and lowest value	28.0	14.0	9.0	16.1	7.7
Coefficient of variation[1]	86.2	59.7	91.3	119.4	94.7

Source: International Monetary Fund, *International Financial Statistics,* various issues.
[1]Absolute value of standard deviation divided by mean and multiplied by 100.

Table 21. Changes in Relative Consumer Prices Adjusted for Exchange Rate Developments in ERM Countries, First Quarter 1979–First Quarter 1990[1]

(In percentage points)

	Belgium	Denmark	France	Germany, Fed. Rep. of	Ireland	Italy	Netherlands
Belgium	—	−15.5	−13.4	−8.4	−31.5	−35.4	−3.4
Denmark	18.4	—	2.5	8.4	−18.9	−23.5	14.4
France	15.5	−2.4	—	5.8	−20.9	−25.3	11.6
Germany, Fed. Rep. of	9.2	−7.7	−5.5	—	−25.2	−29.4	5.5
Ireland	46.0	23.3	26.4	33.7	—	−5.6	41.1
Italy	54.7	30.7	33.9	41.7	6.0	—	49.5
Netherlands	3.5	−12.6	−10.4	−5.2	−29.1	−33.1	—

Sources: International Monetary Fund, *International Financial Statistics,* and staff calculations.

[1]The figures indicate the difference in consumer price inflation rates adjusted for exchange rate changes between the row and the column country. A positive number thus indicates a greater rate of price increase in a common currency in the row country than in the respective column country. A devaluation would lower all the figures in the row of the devaluing country.

Table 22.   Changes in Relative Normalized Unit Labor Costs Adjusted for Exchange Rate Developments in ERM Countries, First Quarter 1979–First Quarter 1990[1]

(In percentage points)

	Belgium	Denmark	France	Germany, Fed. Rep. of	Ireland	Italy	Netherlands
Belgium	—	−26.7	−29.5	−35.6	−31.6	−45.9	−14.4
Denmark	36.3	—	−3.9	−12.2	−6.8	−26.3	16.8
France	41.9	4.1	—	−8.6	−2.9	−23.2	21.5
Germany, Fed. Rep. of	55.2	13.9	9.4	—	6.2	−16.0	32.9
Ireland	46.2	7.3	3.0	−5.8	—	−20.9	25.2
Italy	84.9	35.6	30.3	19.1	26.4	—	58.3
Netherlands	16.8	−14.3	−17.7	−24.8	−20.1	−36.8	—

Sources: International Monetary Fund, *International Financial Statistics,* and staff calculations.

[1]The figures indicate the difference in changes in normalized unit labor costs in manufacturing adjusted for exchange rate changes between the row and the column country. A positive number thus indicates a greater rate of increase in a common currency in the row country than in the respective column country. A devaluation would lower all the figures in the row of the devaluing country.

Table 23. Changes in Relative Value-Added Deflators in Manufacturing Adjusted for Exchange Rate Developments in ERM Countries, First Quarter 1979–First Quarter 1990[1]

(In percentage points)

	Belgium	Denmark	France	Germany, Fed. Rep. of	Ireland	Italy	Netherlands
Belgium	—	−36.2	−30.1	−32.6	−41.0	−40.2	−24.6
Denmark	56.7	—	9.5	5.6	−7.5	−6.3	18.2
France	43.1	−8.7	—	−3.6	−15.5	−14.4	7.9
Germany, Fed. Rep. of	48.4	−5.3	3.7	—	−12.4	−11.2	12.0
Ireland	69.4	8.1	18.4	14.2	—	1.3	27.8
Italy	67.2	6.7	16.9	12.7	−1.3	—	26.2
Netherlands	32.5	−15.4	−7.4	−10.7	−21.8	−20.7	—

Sources: International Monetary Fund, *International Financial Statistics,* and staff calculations.

[1]The figures indicate the difference in changes in value-added deflators in manufacturing adjusted for exchange rate changes between the row and the column country. A positive number thus indicates a greater rate of increase in a common currency in the row country than in the respective column country. A devaluation would lower all the figures in the row of the devaluing country.

Table 24. Real Effective Exchange Rates Relative to Federal Republic of Germany, 1975–88[1]

(1985 = 100)

	1975–78	1979–82	1983–86	1987	1988
Belgium	135.2	121.4	98.9	87.7	82.4
Denmark	125.4	105.7	98.1	100.3	97.5
France	100.4	99.6	97.2	86.3	82.9
Ireland	102.6	101.4	99.9	90.2	85.8
Italy	86.7	86.6	96.8	89.3	88.6
Netherlands	118.3	106.2	100.3	93.4	90.6
Average ERM	111.4	103.5	98.5	91.2	86.1
Austria	108.2	100.3	100.5	96.5	95.0
Norway	87.6	86.0	96.0	89.8	92.1
Spain	84.3	108.1	98.1	92.8	98.8
Sweden	113.4	100.7	93.5	87.5	90.7
Switzerland	100.9	98.2	101.9	97.8	96.9
United Kingdom	70.3	96.8	96.2	83.7	94.1
Average other Europe	94.1	98.4	97.7	91.4	94.6
Canada	99.4	91.2	98.1	82.6	90.4
Japan	102.9	97.3	103.0	107.8	116.1
United States	69.9	70.7	89.3	61.4	58.0
Average other industrial countries	90.7	86.4	96.8	83.9	88.2
Average non-ERM	93.0	94.4	97.4	88.9	92.4

Source: International Monetary Fund, *International Financial Statistics*, various issues.

[1]Based on normalized unit labor costs.

Table 25. Evolution of Export Market Shares, 1979–88

(Annual percentage change)

	1979	1980	1981	1982	1983	1984	1985	1986	1987	1988	Cumulative Growth, 1979–88[1]
Belgium											
Volume of exports[2]	4.6	1.5	1.2	1.7	4.1	5.5	5.3	6.9	8.5	9.2	160.1
Market growth[3]	7.5	4.9	2.4	3.3	4.4	7.9	4.5	4.5	5.9	5.7	164.3
Export market share[4]	−2.7	−3.3	−1.2	−1.5	−0.3	−2.2	0.7	2.3	2.4	3.3	97.4
Denmark											
Volume of exports[2]	9.1	11.0	7.8	2.4	5.2	5.3	5.2	0.1	1.8	5.5	167.5
Market growth[3]	8.4	3.9	1.4	3.4	5.0	9.9	5.5	5.4	6.5	7.5	173.5
Export market share[4]	0.6	6.8	6.3	−1.0	0.2	−4.2	−0.3	−5.0	−4.4	−1.9	96.5
France											
Volume of exports[2]	8.8	3.7	4.6	−3.7	4.7	4.9	1.6	−0.1	2.7	8.8	141.6
Market growth[3]	6.7	4.8	2.9	1.7	2.8	7.8	3.2	3.2	5.6	7.5	156.8
Export market share[4]	2.0	−1.0	1.7	−5.3	1.9	−2.7	−1.6	−3.2	−2.7	1.2	90.3
Germany, Fed. Rep. of											
Volume of exports[2]	4.8	1.7	6.7	3.4	−0.3	9.4	6.0	1.2	3.1	7.1	151.9
Market growth[3]	7.6	5.0	2.7	2.1	3.4	9.2	4.8	4.6	6.3	8.2	168.7
Export market share[4]	−2.6	−3.1	3.9	1.3	−3.6	0.2	1.1	−3.3	−3.0	−1.0	90.0
Ireland											
Volume of exports[2]	8.2	7.6	0.9	7.2	12.1	18.3	6.5	3.4	14.4	11.0	233.5
Market growth[3]	9.5	2.1	−0.5	3.9	7.6	7.1	7.4	6.8	8.3	11.0	183.7
Export market share[4]	4.3	5.8	1.4	3.2	4.2	10.5	−0.8	−3.2	5.6	—	127.1
Italy											
Volume of exports[2]	9.5	−5.1	6.9	−2.4	4.9	8.9	3.0	3.4	3.7	5.7	144.6
Market growth[3]	7.4	4.5	2.6	2.8	4.2	8.2	5.0	5.2	6.6	8.3	170.2
Export market share[4]	2.0	−9.2	4.2	−5.1	0.7	0.6	−1.9	−1.7	−2.7	−2.4	85.0
Netherlands											
Volume of exports[2]	10.9	2.6	2.6	−1.6	4.1	8.5	6.2	1.1	4.8	10.6	161.5
Market growth[3]	7.7	4.0	1.4	2.8	3.9	7.3	4.3	4.9	5.9	6.4	160.5
Export market share[4]	3.0	−1.3	1.2	−4.3	0.3	1.1	1.8	−3.6	−1.0	3.9	100.6
Memorandum items:											
United Kingdom											
Volume of exports[2]	0.1	1.7	−4.0	1.2	0.5	7.6	5.4	4.0	6.8	3.2	129.2
Market growth[3]	6.6	4.8	5.1	1.9	3.5	9.3	3.5	3.2	6.0	7.5	164.7
Export market share[4]	−6.1	−3.0	−8.7	−0.7	−2.9	−1.6	1.8	0.8	0.8	−4.0	78.4
Japan											
Volume of exports[2]	−0.8	19.2	11.5	−2.4	8.0	15.7	5.1	−0.5	0.4	4.3	176.1
Market growth[3]	7.0	4.9	7.5	1.2	8.8	15.0	5.0	4.6	7.8	9.6	198.3
Export market share[4]	−7.3	13.6	3.7	−3.6	−0.7	0.6	0.1	−4.9	−6.9	−4.8	88.8
Spain											
Volume of exports[2]	13.5	1.0	6.5	1.3	6.5	16.7	1.7	−7.9	7.7	9.5	169.8
Market growth[3]	7.2	6.9	5.0	1.9	2.8	8.0	2.9	2.1	5.1	7.0	160.8
Export market share[4]	5.9	−5.5	1.4	−0.6	3.6	8.1	−1.2	−9.8	2.5	2.3	105.6

Sources: International Monetary Fund, *World Economic Outlook;* Research Department, *Selected Indicators of Demand and Output;* and staff estimates.

[1]1979 = 100.

[2]Non-oil merchandise exports, customs basis.

[3]Non-oil imports in partner countries, trade-weighted.

[4]Ratio of export volume growth to market growth.

Table 26. Broad Money, 1975–89

(Annual change in percent)

	1975–78	1979–82	1983–86	1987	1988	1989
Belgium	10.9	5.7	7.1	9.1	5.3	10.7
Denmark	13.6	11.0	18.2	6.5	5.5	1.3
France	28.8	11.3	8.5	6.5	5.6	4.8
Germany, Fed. Rep. of	9.9	5.1	6.5	6.0	5.8	5.1
Ireland	19.7	12.9	9.2	8.8	6.5	14.0
Italy	22.2	15.4	11.3	8.6	8.8	11.6
Netherlands	13.5	7.4	5.9	1.9	7.4	10.2
Average ERM	16.9	9.8	9.5	6.8	6.6	9.4
Standard deviation	6.4	3.6	3.9	2.3	1.2	3.4
Difference between highest and lowest value	18.9	10.3	12.3	7.2	3.4	9.2
Coefficient of variation[1]	37.7	36.3	41.4	34.3	18.3	36.0
Austria	14.7	10.5	6.5	7.5	5.8	7.8
Norway	13.2	12.2	11.8	19.2	4.9	8.4
Spain	19.3	16.1	8.1	9.2	15.1	9.9
Sweden	10.9	12.1	12.7	5.0	8.4	10.9
Switzerland	8.7	8.5	6.4	10.5	5.4	6.3
United Kingdom	10.7	17.5	13.9	92.1	17.4	19.4
Average other Europe	12.9	12.8	9.9	23.9	9.5	10.4
Standard deviation	3.4	3.1	3.0	30.8	5.0	4.3
Difference between highest and lowest value	10.6	9.0	7.5	87.2	12.5	13.2
Coefficient of variation[1]	26.7	24.2	30.2	128.8	52.1	41.1
Australia	12.3	11.5	13.1	16.0	21.3	27.9
Canada	16.4	13.6	4.6	8.7	10.6	13.5
Japan	13.0	8.4	8.0	11.2	9.8	11.8
United States	11.2	6.7	11.0	4.0	6.1	3.8
Average other industrial countries	13.2	10.1	9.2	10.0	12.0	14.2
Standard deviation	1.9	2.7	3.2	4.3	5.7	8.7
Difference between highest and lowest value	5.2	7.0	8.5	12.1	15.2	24.0
Coefficient of variation[1]	14.7	26.9	35.0	43.7	47.3	60.9
Average non-ERM	13.0	11.7	9.6	18.3	10.5	12.0
Standard deviation	2.9	3.2	3.1	25.0	5.4	6.7
Difference between highest and lowest value	10.6	10.9	9.3	88.2	16.4	24.0
Coefficient of variation[1]	22.6	27.7	32.3	136.3	51.3	55.8

Source: International Monetary Fund, *International Financial Statistics,* various issues.

[1]Absolute value of standard deviation divided by mean and multiplied by 100.

Table 27. Velocity of Broad Money, 1975–88

(Annual change in percent)

	1975–78	1979–82	1983–86	1987	1988
Belgium	−1.0	0.7	0.1	−5.1	−2.5
Denmark	−0.8	0.1	−7.5	−2.2	0.0
France	−0.5	2.1	−0.6	−5.5	−3.9
Germany, Fed. Rep. of	−2.3	0.0	−1.4	−2.4	−0.7
Ireland	2.1	2.4	−1.1	−1.9	−2.6
Italy	−1.1	4.6	0.9	0.4	1.6
Netherlands	−3.2	−2.4	−1.9	−2.9	−0.5
Average ERM	−1.0	1.1	−1.6	−2.8	−1.4
Standard deviation	1.5	2.0	2.5	1.9	1.8
Difference between highest and lowest value	5.3	7.0	8.4	5.9	5.4
Coefficient of variation[1]	157.1	188.0	156.6	66.9	123.5
Austria	−5.6	−2.8	−1.0	−3.6	−0.8
Norway	0.2	1.8	−3.2	−1.1	−5.3
Spain	2.2	−1.6	5.2	−0.8	−1.0
Sweden	2.6	−1.8	−1.1	−1.7	2.0
Switzerland	−4.4	−0.8	−1.2	−2.1	−1.9
United Kingdom	7.5	−3.6	−4.7	−10.1	−8.9
Average other Europe	0.4	−1.5	−1.0	−3.2	−2.6
Standard deviation	4.4	1.7	3.1	3.2	3.5
Difference between highest and lowest value	13.1	5.4	9.8	9.3	10.9
Coefficient of variation[1]	1,045.8	114.4	307.4	99.1	132.8
Australia	3.3	2.8	−2.0	−0.4	−4.8
Canada	−3.7	−2.9	3.4	0.9	−0.4
Japan	−1.0	−1.7	−2.3	−5.5	−3.9
United States	0.3	2.3	−3.0	0.4	2.5
Average other industrial countries	−0.3	0.1	−1.0	−1.1	−1.6
Standard deviation	2.5	2.4	2.6	2.5	2.9
Difference between highest and lowest value	7.0	5.6	6.4	6.4	7.2
Coefficient of variation[1]	950.2	1,811.8	266.0	226.2	176.1
Average non-ERM	0.1	−0.8	−1.0	−2.4	−2.2
Standard deviation	3.8	2.2	2.9	3.1	3.3
Difference between highest and lowest value	13.1	6.4	9.8	11.0	11.3
Coefficient of variation[1]	2,572.1	261.2	292.2	131.1	147.7

Source: International Monetary Fund, *International Financial Statistics,* various issues.

[1] Absolute value of standard deviation divided by mean and multiplied by 100.

Table 28. Matrix of Correlation Coefficients Between Short-Term Interest Rates,[1] January 1975–March 1979; April 1979–December 1982; January 1983–December 1986; and January 1987–December 1989

		Belgium	Denmark	France	Germany, Fed. Rep. of	Ireland	Italy
Denmark	January 1975–March 1979	0.31					
	April 1979–December 1982	0.39					
	January 1983–December 1986	0.52					
	January 1987–December 1989	0.59					
France	January 1975–March 1979	0.38	0.42				
	April 1979–December 1982	0.53	0.40				
	January 1983–December 1986	0.42	0.39				
	January 1987–December 1989	0.86	0.62				
Germany, Fed. Rep. of	January 1975–March 1979	−0.03	−0.08	0.46			
	April 1979–December 1982	0.58	0.21	0.72			
	January 1983–December 1986	0.63	0.53	0.63			
	January 1987–December 1989	0.79	0.29	0.82			
Ireland	January 1975–March 1979	—	—	—	—		
	April 1979–December 1982	0.42	0.20	0.40	0.12		
	January 1983–December 1986	0.45	0.49	0.29	0.43		
	January 1987–December 1989	0.55	0.84	0.47	0.14		
Italy	January 1975–March 1979	0.61	0.28	0.61	0.31	—	
	April 1979–December 1982	0.57	0.24	0.80	0.72	0.17	
	January 1983–December 1986	0.61	0.49	0.60	0.69	0.55	
	January 1987–December 1989	0.74	0.29	0.77	0.84	0.20	
Netherlands	January 1975–March 1979	0.63	0.25	0.22	—	—	0.29
	April 1979–December 1982	0.35	0.16	0.38	0.62	0.29	0.15
	January 1983–December 1986	−0.11	−0.31	−0.23	0.92	−0.44	−0.38
	January 1987–December 1989	0.87	0.52	0.90	0.92	0.41	0.83

Source: International Monetary Fund, *International Financial Statistics,* various issues.

[1]Money market rates, line 60b of *International Financial Statistics*.

Table 29.   Matrix of Correlation Coefficients Between Long-Term Interest Rates,[1] January 1975–March 1979; April 1979–December 1982; January 1983–December 1986; and January 1987–December 1989

		Belgium	Denmark	France	Germany, Fed. Rep. of	Ireland	Italy
Denmark	January 1975–March 1979	−0.30					
	April 1979–December 1982	0.78					
	January 1983–December 1986	0.75					
	January 1987–December 1989	−0.28					
France	January 1975–March 1979	0.26	−0.49				
	April 1979–December 1982	0.98	0.82				
	January 1983–December 1986	0.80	0.66				
	January 1987–December 1989	−0.95	0.47				
Germany, Fed. Rep. of	January 1975–March 1979	0.27	−0.34	0.17			
	April 1979–December 1982	0.79	0.47	0.79			
	January 1983–December 1986	0.89	0.72	0.80			
	January 1987–December 1989	0.92	−0.23	−0.20			
Ireland	January 1975–March 1979	0.56	−0.45	0.22	0.72		
	April 1979–December 1982	0.59	0.51	0.62	0.67		
	January 1983–December 1986	0.76	0.75	0.80	0.77		
	January 1987–December 1989	−0.52	0.31	0.47	−0.62		
Italy	January 1975–March 1979	0.23	0.10	0.53	−0.80	−0.32	
	April 1979–December 1982	0.91	0.84	0.95	0.74	0.61	
	January 1983–December 1986	0.84	0.68	0.70	0.82	0.54	
	January 1987–December 1989	0.72	−0.87	0.17	0.73	−0.52	
Netherlands	January 1975–March 1979	0.41	−0.31	0.87	0.81	0.67	−0.43
	April 1979–December 1982	0.76	0.51	0.76	0.94	0.62	0.66
	January 1983–December 1986	0.89	0.74	0.78	0.98	0.72	0.86
	January 1987–December 1989	0.92	−0.26	−0.62	0.94	−0.42	0.72

Source: International Monetary Fund, *International Financial Statistics,* various issues.
[1]Government bond yields, line 61 of *International Financial Statistics.*

Table 30.   Variability of Interest Rates, January 1975–December 1989

(Coefficient of variation)

	January 1975–March 1979		April 1979–December 1982		January 1983–December 1986		January 1987–December 1989	
	Short-term[1]	Long-term[2]	Short-term[1]	Long-term[2]	Short-term[1]	Long-term[2]	Short-term[1]	Long-term[2]
Belgium	37.3	4.0	19.2	12.9	19.4	16.6	19.8	6.2
Denmark	43.9	10.0	24.3	10.6	23.6	15.3	13.1	8.1
France	15.9	6.0	22.2	17.6	31.9	31.2	10.1	5.9
Germany, Fed. Rep. of	21.6	16.7	21.1	12.5	9.5	12.2	30.5	9.8
Ireland	56.7	11.9	13.3	9.3	16.6	13.2	21.2	12.0
Italy	22.5	8.9	18.1	16.6	14.2	20.7	6.4	6.9
Netherlands	60.7	7.3	20.2	10.4	9.1	12.5	23.0	7.5

Source: International Monetary Fund, *International Financial Statistics,* various issues.

[1]Money market rates, line 60b of *International Financial Statistics.*

[2]Government bond yields, line 61 of *International Financial Statistics.*

Table 31. General Government Budget Balances, 1975–87

(In percent of GDP/GNP)

	1975–78	1979–82	1983	1984	1985	1986	1987
Belgium	−1.5	−5.8	−8.1	−6.3	−6.1	−6.6	−5.1
Denmark	−0.6	−5.2	−7.2	−4.1	−2.0	3.5	2.0
France	−1.5	−1.4	−3.2	−2.8	−2.8	−2.9	−2.4
Germany, Fed. Rep. of	−3.5	−3.1	−2.5	−1.9	−1.1	−1.3	−1.8
Ireland	−8.4	−12.2	−12.5	−10.5	−12.2	−12.1	0.0
Italy	0.0	−10.4	−10.6	−11.6	−12.5	−11.7	−11.2
Netherlands	−2.5	−5.1	−6.3	−6.3	−4.7	−5.9	−6.2
Average ERM	−2.6	−6.2	−7.2	−6.2	−5.9	−5.3	−4.1
Standard deviation	2.6	3.6	3.4	3.4	4.4	5.2	4.1
Difference between highest and lowest value	8.4	10.8	10.0	9.7	11.4	15.5	13.2
Coefficient of variation[1]	100.6	57.5	46.6	55.3	73.4	98.0	99.7
Austria	−2.8	−2.3	−4.0	−2.6	−2.5	−3.7	−4.1
Norway	1.7	4.0	4.2	7.4	10.2	5.5	3.4
Spain	0.0	−3.0	−4.8	−5.5	−7.0	−6.1	0.0
Sweden	2.1	−4.5	−5.0	−2.6	−3.8	−0.6	4.1
United Kingdom	−4.3	−3.4	−3.4	−3.8	−2.9	−3.0	0.0
Average other Europe	−0.7	−1.8	−2.6	−1.4	−1.2	−1.6	1.1
Standard deviation	2.5	3.0	3.4	4.6	5.9	3.9	3.7
Difference between highest and lowest value	6.5	8.5	9.2	12.9	17.2	11.6	8.2
Coefficient of variation[1]	382.3	164.5	132.6	323.7	498.6	248.7	331.3
Australia	−2.7	−1.3	−3.8	−3.3	−2.9	−1.5	0.3
Canada	−2.5	−3.0	−6.9	−6.5	−7.0	−5.4	−4.6
Japan	−3.9	−4.1	−3.7	−2.1	−0.8	−0.9	0.6
United States	−2.0	−1.6	−4.8	−3.8	−4.1	−4.3	−3.5
Average other industrial countries	−2.8	−2.5	−4.8	−3.9	−3.7	−3.1	−1.8
Standard deviation	0.7	1.2	1.3	1.6	2.2	1.9	2.3
Difference between highest and lowest value	1.9	2.8	3.3	4.4	6.2	4.5	5.2
Coefficient of variation[1]	25.4	45.7	26.9	41.0	60.6	61.1	127.4
Average non-ERM	−1.6	−2.1	−3.6	−2.5	−2.3	−2.2	−0.5
Standard deviation	2.2	2.4	2.9	3.8	4.8	3.3	3.3
Difference between highest and lowest value	6.5	8.5	11.1	13.9	17.2	11.6	8.6
Coefficient of variation[1]	137.7	112.2	81.6	149.5	208.7	146.1	616.1

Source: Organization for Economic Cooperation and Development, *National Accounts Statistics* (Paris, 1989).

[1]Absolute value of standard deviation divided by mean and multiplied by 100.

Table 32.   Real Growth and Unemployment, 1971–89

(In percent)

	1971–80	1981–86	1987	1988	1989[1]
GDP growth					
Belgium	3.2	0.9	2.0	4.0	4.2
Denmark	2.2	2.8	−1.0	−0.4	1.6
France	3.3	1.6	2.2	3.4	3.3
Germany, Fed. Rep. of	2.7	1.4	1.9	3.7	3.8
Ireland	4.5	1.8	4.1	3.7	5.1
Italy	3.1	1.9	3.1	3.9	3.5
Netherlands	2.9	1.2	1.3	2.8	3.8
EC	2.9	1.7	2.8	3.8	3.4
Unemployment					
Belgium	4.9	11.8	11.5	10.4	9.4
Denmark	4.6	8.9	5.8	6.4	7.4
France	4.3	9.1	10.5	10.2	9.5
Germany, Fed. Rep. of	2.7	6.6	6.4	6.4	5.6
Ireland	7.1	15.1	18.0	17.8	16.7
Italy	6.6	9.2	10.1	10.6	10.5
Netherlands	4.2	11.0	10.2	10.3	9.9
EC	4.4	10.0	10.4	10.0	9.0

Source: Commission of the European Communities, "Annual Economic Report, 1989–90," *European Economy*, No. 42 (November 1989).
[1]Estimate.

Appendix II
Press Communiqués

Committee of Governors of the Central Banks of the Member States of the European Economic Community

Press Communiqué

September 18, 1987

At their monthly meeting on 8 September 1987, the Governors of the Central Banks of the Member States of the European Economic Community agreed on measures to strengthen the operating mechanisms of the European Monetary System, which are as follows:

1. The duration of the very short-term financing on which central banks can draw through the European Monetary Cooperation Fund (EMCF) to finance interventions in EMS currencies will be extended by one month, taking the maximum duration from two and a half to three and a half months. The ceiling applied to the automatic renewal for three months of these financing operations will be doubled, i.e., it will amount to 200 percent of the central bank's debtor quota in the short-term monetary support mechanism instead of 100 percent as at present.

2. The Governors point out that very short-term financing through the EMCF of intramarginal interventions in EMS currencies is already possible if the central banks directly involved concur. While there will be no automatic access to such financing, a presumption that intramarginal interventions in EMS currencies agreed to by the central bank issuing the intervention currency will qualify for very short-term financing via the EMCF will be established under certain conditions; the cumulative amount of such financing made available to the debtor central bank shall not exceed 200 percent of its debtor quota in the short-term monetary support mechanism, the debtor central bank is also prepared to use its holdings of the currency to be sold in amounts to be agreed and the creditor central bank may request repayment in its own currency taking into account the reserve position of the debtor central bank.

3. The usability of the official ECU will be further enhanced. The central banks will accept settlements in ECUs of outstanding claims in the very short-term financing in excess of their obligation (50 percent) and up to 100 percent as long as this does not result in an unbalanced composition of reserves and no excessive debtor and creditor positions in ECUs arise. After two years of experience, the formal rules relating to the official ECU will be subject to review.

These measures form part of a comprehensive strategy to foster exchange rate cohesion within the EMS. The Governors are convinced that greater exchange rate stability depends on all Member States achieving, through their economic and monetary policies, sufficient convergence towards internal stability. In the light of this basic understanding they have agreed in particular to exploit the scope for a more active, flexible and concerted use of the instruments available, namely, exchange rate movements within the fluctuation band, interest rates and interventions. To promote this more effective use of the instruments, the Committee of Governors will strengthen the procedure for joint monitoring of economic and monetary developments and policies with the aim of arriving at common assessments of both the prevailing conjuncture and appropriate policy responses.

This strategy and these measures were presented by the Governors to the EEC Ministers of Finance at the informal meeting in Nyborg on 12 September 1987. The changes to the operating mechanisms of the EMS will come into effect following the formal amendment of certain provisions of the central bank Agreement of 13 March 1979 which lays down the operating procedures for the EMS and consequential changes to the rules governing the operations of the European Monetary Cooperation Fund which will take place in the coming weeks.

EC Ministers of Economics and Finance

Communiqué

September 12, 1987

At their informal meeting in Nyborg, Denmark, on 12 September, the Ministers of Economics and Finance agreed on a series of moves to strengthen the EMS and fully concurred with the measures agreed earlier by the central bank Governors in Basle.

The strengthening of the EMS should be seen in the light of the much improved, but by no means perfect, convergence of economic policies and performances in the Community, as well as of the risks posed to the cohesion of the System by the Community's move towards full capital liberalization.

The set of measures agreed by Ministers and Governors to strengthen the EMS fall into two main categories:

A. Measures designed to increase convergence and avoid conflicting policies which would threaten the cohesion of the System:

—A six-monthly Monetary Committee surveillance procedure using economic indicators and projections (in line with the G-7 framework) will be carried out, designed to highlight any policy inconsistencies between EMS countries and incompatible approaches to third currencies.

—A Monetary Committee monthly examination of the latest exchange and interest rate developments has been set up to consider what conclusions can be drawn.

—A Committee of Governors monthly monitoring procedure will take place, focusing on simultaneous consideration of intervention, exchange rate and interest rate policies to discuss appropriate policy responses regarding not only EMS currencies but also third currencies and the ECU.

These procedural improvements are backed by a consensus to lay emphasis on the use of interest rate differentials to defend the stability of the EMS parity grid, to use the permitted fluctuation margins flexibly in order to deter speculation and to avoid prolonged bouts of intramarginal intervention; also realignments should be infrequent and as small as possible. With respect to third currencies, since their movements can cause disturbances in the EMS, any potential incom-

patible approaches involving major third currencies will be kept under close review.

B. Measures to improve the intervention mechanism of the EMS:

—In the future, there will be a presumption that the very short-term financing (VSTF) facility shall be available within specified limits[1] for intramarginal interventions. Up to now VSTF use via the European Monetary Cooperation Fund (EMCF), under which the intervening central bank borrows a strong currency from the issuing central bank for intervention purposes, has only been available when the currencies are at their margins and intervention is obligatory, at which point VSTF financing is automatic. In the past, intramarginal intervention has normally been funded by the weak currency central bank from its reserves, usually of DM, subject to the accord of the other central bank concerned which was generally forthcoming. Under the new formula the permission of the central bank issuing the intervention currency will still be required for intramarginal intervention, but there will be a presumption that intramarginal intervention agreed to will qualify for the VSTF facility within the abovementioned limits and subject, when appropriate, to certain conditions (concurrent use of own reserves, reimbursement in the creditor's currency).

—The duration of the VSTF facility will be extended by one month, taking the maximum duration from two and a half to three and a half months. The initial financing operation will still be automatically renewable for a further three months, but the ceiling on automatic renewal will be doubled to twice the debtor quota in the STMS mechanism.

—The acceptance limit for settlement in official ecus of VSTF debts has been raised from 50 percent to 100 percent for a trial period of two years.

The presumption of VSTF availability for intramarginal interventions is potentially by far the most important of the above category of measures, but its impact will have to be seen in the light of experience since it is not automatic. The availability of the VSTF facility will "officialize" intramarginal intervention, which was not explicitly foreseen in the original EMS texts,

---

[1] The limits are double the debtor quota of the short-term monetary support (STMS) mechanism (Germany, France: ECU 3,480 million; Italy: ECU 2,320 million; Belgium, the Netherlands: ECU 1,160 million; Denmark: ECU 520 million; Ireland: ECU 200 million).

but which has become standard practice. It will become more symmetric in its monetary effect in the strong and weak currency countries and it will add to the central banks' defenses against speculative capital movements. Extending the duration for the VSTF and raising the ceiling on its renewal takes account of the larger capital flows and the tendency for these flows to take longer to reverse in the context of small realignments. The raising of the official ECU acceptance limit will add to the usability of the official ECU which at present effectively provides a way of using dollar and gold reserves for credit against Community currencies; it will thus in practice enlarge the potential funds available for intervention purposes.

This agreement marks a substantial step forward for monetary cooperation in the Community. It constitutes the beginning of a new phase for the EMS, creating in a flexible way a better-balanced System while maintaining the primary objective of establishing a greater degree of internal (prices) and external (exchange rates) stability in Europe. The agreement incorporates the G-7 indicator exercise, adapting it to EMS circumstances by laying more emphasis on the maintenance of exchange rate stability, and thereby takes account of international discussions.

Excerpts from Conclusions of the Presidency, European Council, Rome, October 27 and 28, 1990

Conference on Economic and Monetary Union

The European Council in Madrid fixed the date for the start of the first phase of economic and monetary union; in Strasbourg and Dublin it set the timetable for the Intergovernmental Conference and the ratification of its results. It now notes with satisfaction the important developments that have occurred in the wake of these decisions.

The European Council takes note of the results of the preparatory work that constitutes the basis for the Intergovernmental Conference.

For the final phase of economic and monetary union eleven member states consider that the work on the amendment of the Treaty will be directed to the following points:

—for economic union, an open market system, that combines price stability with growth, employment, and environmental protection; and is dedicated to sound and sustainable financial and budgetary conditions and to economic and social cohe-

sion. To this end, the ability to act of the Community institutions will be strengthened;
—for monetary union, the creation of a new monetary institution comprising Member States' central banks and a central organ, exercising full responsibility for monetary policy. The monetary institution's prime task will be to maintain price stability; without prejudice to this objective, it will support the general economic policy of the Community. The institution as such, as well as the members of its Council, will be independent of instructions. It will report to the institutions which are politically responsible.

With the achievement of the final phase of economic and monetary union, exchange rates will be irrevocably fixed. The Community will have a single currency—a strong and stable ECU—which will be an expression of its identity and unity. During the transitional phase, the ECU will be further strengthened and developed.

The second phase will start on 1 January 1994 after:
—the single market program has been achieved;
—the Treaty has been ratified; and, by its provisions:
—a process has been set in train designed to ensure the independence of the members of the new monetary institution at the latest when monetary powers have been transferred;
—the monetary financing of budget deficits has been prohibited and any responsibility on the part of the Community or its Member States for one Member State's debt precluded;
—the greatest possible number of Member States have adhered to the exchange rate mechanism.

The European Council recalls that, in order to move on to the second phase, further satisfactory and lasting progress toward real and monetary convergence will have to be achieved, especially as regards price stability and the restoration of sound public finances.

At the start of the second phase, the new Community institution will be established. This will make it possible, in particular:

—to strengthen the coordination of monetary policies;
—to develop the instruments and procedures needed for the future conduct of a single monetary policy;
—to oversee the development of the ECU.

At the latest within three years from the start of the second phase, the Commission and the Council of the monetary institution will report to the ECOFIN Council and to the General Affairs Council on the functioning of the second phase and in particular on the progress made in real convergence, in order to prepare the decision concerning the passage to the third phase, which will occur within a reasonable time. The General Affairs Council will submit the dossier to the European Council.

The Treaty may lay down transitional provisions for the successive stages of economic and monetary union according to the circumstances of the different countries.

The United Kingdom is unable to accept the approach set out above. But it agrees that the overriding objective of monetary policy should be price stability, that the Community's development should be based on an open market system, that excessive budget deficits should be avoided, and that there should be no monetary financing of deficits nor the assumption of responsibility on the part of the Community or its Member States for one Member State's debts. The United Kingdom, while ready to move beyond stage one through the creation of a new monetary institution and a common Community currency, believes that decisions on the substance of that move should precede decisions on its timing. But it would be ready to see the approach it advocates come into affect as soon as possible after ratification of the necessary Treaty provision. . . .

Appendix III
Chronology of EC Monetary and Financial Integration[1]

April 1948: Establishment of Organization for European Economic Cooperation (OEEC).

May 1950: French Minister of Foreign Affairs Robert Schuman proposes creation of an organization governing European production/consumption of coal and steel. Calls for a "High Authority" to oversee new organization. Goal is to integrate the economies of France and the Federal Republic of Germany—although open to all European countries.

September 19, 1950: Agreement establishing the European Payments Union (EPU) in the framework of the OEEC signed. The EPU established to reduce bilateralism in trade and payments in Europe and to prevent the postwar shortage of dollars from limiting European trade. The EPU administered by the Bank for International Settlements and supported in part by a capital fund from the United States to serve as a buffer against defaults or payment delays.

April 1951: France, the Federal Republic of Germany, Italy, Belgium, the Netherlands, and Luxembourg sign the Treaty of Paris, establishing the European Coal and Steel Community (ECSC). Parliaments ratify the treaty in winter 1951–spring 1952; the United Kingdom declines membership.

May 1952: The six sign treaty for European Defence Community (EDC), and plan for European Political Community.

August 1954: French National Assembly rejects EDC.

June 1955: Intergovernmental committee, headed by Belgian Paul-Henri Spaak, set up to pursue economic union and union in nuclear energy.

May 1956: Spaak Report approved in Venice—talk begins of economic union among the six and others. As talk of "common" policies increases, United Kingdom declines to participate and proposes European free trade area in October 1956.

March 25, 1957: The six sign Treaties of Rome, establishing European Economic Community (EEC), including European Investment Bank (EIB), and European Atomic Energy Community (Euratom). Together with the ECSC, they form the European Communities (EC). Parliaments ratify within a few months. Stated objectives are customs union with free movement of goods, ending trade quotas and barriers; free movement of services and capital. Also, to provide common policies in international trade, agriculture, transport, and social matters. Foreign and defense policies to remain under control of member states.

January 1, 1958: EEC and Euratom treaties take effect. By spring, respective Councils of Ministers and Commissions are in place.

March 1958: EEC Council decision drawing up rules governing the Monetary Committee established by EEC Article 105. Committee to review the monetary and financial situation in the member states and Community as a whole and to review system of currency payments in the Community.

March 19–21, 1958: Constituting session of European Parliament.

December 1958: West European countries restore convertibility of their currencies under IMF Articles of Agreement. End of European Payments Union. Succeeded by European Monetary Agreement.

January 1959: First cut in customs duties in trade between EEC member states. All customs duties—excluding agricultural products—to be eliminated in intra-EEC trade by 1969.

June–July 1959: Greece and Turkey apply to become associated states.

May 1960: European Free Trade Association (EFTA) is formed—Austria, Denmark, Norway, Portugal, Sweden, Switzerland, and the United Kingdom, with Finland as an associate member. Iceland joins in 1971; Denmark and the United Kingdom leave in 1972; Finland becomes full member in 1986.

---

[1]The chronology was originally prepared by Peter Flanagan for Garry J. Schinasi's paper, *European Integration, Exchange Rate Management, and Monetary Reform: A Review of the Major Issues,* International Finance Discussion Paper No. 364, Board of Governors of the Federal Reserve System, October 1989. It was updated by Mr. Schinasi.

May 1960: EEC Council adopts directive to free certain capital movements in the Community.

July 1961: Greece and EC sign association agreement.

July–August 1961: Denmark, Ireland, Norway, and the United Kingdom apply for EC membership.

September 1961: First regulation on free movement of workers comes into force.

January 1962: Common Agricultural Policy (CAP) starts. Based on single market and prices for most products; preservation of comparable living standards for agricultural workers and workers in other sectors; preferences for Community products; establishment of European Agricultural Guidance and Guarantee Fund (EAGGF) to support objectives of CAP.

February–May 1962: Spain and Portugal request EC association.

October 1962: Commission submits plan to Council for increasing financial consultation and coordination of monetary/economic policies. Call for finance ministers to meet periodically with central bank governors in an effort to increase coordination. Commission proposes three stages to monetary union by 1971, including the creation of a Council of Governors of Central Banks to intensify monetary cooperation. Germany objects, fearing excess liquidity and interference with transatlantic cooperation; par value system of IMF considered to be working well.

January 1963: Negotiations on accession of Denmark, Ireland, Norway, and the United Kingdom break down.

January 1963: France and Germany sign friendship and cooperation agreement.

July 1963: Signing of treaty of association between EC and 18 African countries, including Madagascar (First Yaoundé Convention).

September 1963: Turkey and EC sign association agreement.

May 1964: GATT Kennedy Round begins; results in 35–40 percent cut in EC external tariffs, excluding agricultural products. Signed in June 1967.

April–May 1964: Committee of Governors of Central Banks of the EEC is set up—to review credit policies and confer on monetary measures before implementation. Member states asked to consult before changing exchange rate parities. Budgetary Policy Committee is set up, as well as Medium-Term Economic Policy Committee.

March–June 1965: EEC Commission presents new plan to finance CAP—to give the Community its "own resources" by allocating to the EEC the levies charged at Community's borders on nonmember imports. France opposes, and political rift forms. Overcome in January 1966 with Luxembourg agreement establishing unanimity rule in Council.

May 1967: The United Kingdom, Ireland, Denmark, and Norway reapply to join the EC.

July 1967: Merger of institutions of the three Communities (ECSC, EEC, and Euratom) into a single Council of Ministers and a single Commission.

July 1, 1968: EC customs union is completed, 18 months ahead of the 12-year schedule in the EEC Treaty. All customs duties are removed in intra-Community trade, and common external tariff is established.

February 1969: The Commission's memo on the coordination of economic/monetary policies—the Barre Report—is issued. It emphasizes the need for compatible medium-term policies. Establishes proposals for short-term monetary support and medium-term financial assistance facilities for the Community.

July 1969: The Council supports much of the Barre Report, calling for increased consultations among member states before short-term policy shifts likely to affect other members considerably and approving in principle the establishment of short-term monetary support facility.

December 1–2, 1969: Summit of EC heads of state and government in The Hague calls for establishing economic and monetary union in stages, based on the Barre Report. Committee is formed in March 1970, headed by Pierre Werner, Prime Minister of Luxembourg.

February 1970: Governors of EC central banks agree to system of short-term monetary support. Currently available to all EC central banks, regardless of whether currencies are participating in the EMS exchange rate mechanism.

April 1970: Further reform of Community's own resources. Community to receive all customs duties on nonmember imports, all levies on agricultural imports, and resources from value-added tax calculated by a rate of up to 1 percent of a uniform base.

June 1970: EC Council approves conclusions of interim report of Werner Committee.

October 1970: Final version of Werner Report establishes a program for the creation in stages of an economic and monetary union by 1980. Envisages a union with (1) a single Community currency, or de facto single currency, with member currencies at irreversibly fixed exchange rates (with gradual narrowing of margins); (2) complete liberalization of capital movements within the Community; (3) common central banking system, organized like the U.S. Federal Reserve System, involving common management of internal and external monetary policies; (4) centralized economic policy-making body politically responsible to the European Parliament; and (5) fiscal policy coordination.

March 1971: Medium-term financial assistance facility is set up. Funds are to come from member states, and decisions to be taken by finance ministers.

March 1971: The Council adopts a resolution on the gradual achievement by 1980 of economic and monetary union. Outlines steps to be taken in an initial three-year program, including narrowing the margins of fluctuation among EC currencies, and draws up plans for a European Monetary Cooperation Fund. Implementation is disrupted by the monetary crises of 1971. In May 1971, the floating of the deutsche mark and the Netherlands guilder; in August 1971, the United States suspends convertibility of the dollar into gold, jeopardizing the Bretton Woods system.

December 1971: Smithsonian Agreement reached in Group of Ten to realign participants' exchange rates, endorsed by IMF Executive Board action immediately thereafter. Under the IMF decision on central rates and wider margins, the spread between market rates of two currencies could be as wide as 4½ percent.

January 1972: Treaties are signed for the accession to EC of Denmark, Ireland, Norway, and the United Kingdom. Rapidly ratified by all except Norway, where accession treaty is defeated in referendum. Community of nine effective January 1, 1973.

March 1972: European common margins arrangement ("snake") is instituted, a year before the final collapse of Bretton Woods system. Involves maintaining narrow margins of exchange rate fluctuations around pegged rates among EC currencies, while maintaining fixed—but wider—margins against the dollar. Exchange rates among snake currencies to fluctuate in a 2¼ percent band (the snake), while the whole group would fluctuate within a 4½ percent band against the dollar (the "tunnel," established by the Smithsonian Agreement of December 1971). When superseded by the EMS in March 1979, the deutsche mark, Netherlands guilder, Belgian-Luxembourg francs, and the Danish krone still in the snake. At various times, France, Italy, the United Kingdom, Ireland, Norway, and Sweden participate in, or associate their currencies with, the snake.

March 1973: With move to floating exchange rates, defined margins for EC exchange rates against the dollar (the "tunnel") end.

April 1973: European Monetary Cooperation Fund is established by the Council of Ministers. Referred to as EMCF or FECOM (the French initials), it administers short-term central bank credit facilities; later, the very short-term facility of the EMS and issues the ECU (European currency unit).

February 1974: "Convergence Decision" is taken by the Council of Ministers, calling for increased convergence of economic policies among EC member states. Requires the Council to draw up annual policy guidelines for member states. Passes "Stability Directive" at the same time, requiring members to adopt necessary legislation to allow authorities to accelerate or slow government spending, to control debt of governmental agencies, and to modify direct or indirect taxes.

1974: Drive to economic and monetary union is slowed by national concerns over oil crisis.

1975: European unit of account (EUA) is introduced, based on a basket of EC currencies.

February 1975: Regulation adopted by Council of Ministers establishes the Community loan mechanism (CLM) authorizing the Community itself to borrow funds directly from third countries, from public and private institutions, or in capital markets—with the aim of relending the money to one or more members to help them overcome balance of payments problems caused by oil price shifts.

December 1975: Leo Tindemans, Belgian Prime Minister, presents his report on European Union to EC governments. Report is never acted on by European Council.

1976: EUA is adopted as unit of account for the European Coal and Steel Community.

1977: Directive is adopted harmonizing the value-added tax base for member states.

1978: EUA first used for EC budgets.

July 1978: EC heads of state and government (European Council) meet in Bremen, Germany, and agree on an outline for the European Monetary System (EMS); the goal is "a zone of monetary stability in Europe."

December 5, 1978: European Council adopts a resolution on establishment of the EMS.

March 13, 1979: The EMS comes into force with an agreement between the EC central banks. All EC countries become members of the EMS but the United Kingdom does not participate in the exchange rate mechanism (ERM). Greece as well as Spain and Portugal join the EMS in 1981 and 1986, respectively, after joining the EC, but initially do not participate in the ERM. Spain enters the ERM in June 1989, and the United Kingdom in October 1990. Since the creation of the EMS, there have been 12 realignments, the most recent on January 8, 1990. Creation of ECU, based on same basket of currencies as EUA.

May 1979: Greece signs Treaty of Accession; becomes the tenth EC member on January 1, 1981.

May 1980: Temporary solution is reached on debate over U.K. budget rebate. The United Kingdom's contribution to the Community's budget is viewed as too large a burden, given the benefits the country receives. Budget contribution is reduced for 1980 and 1981.

January 1981: The ECU replaces the EUA in the Community's general budget.

March 1984: Council of Ministers agrees to package of reforms for Common Agricultural Policy, including a new pricing policy, guarantee thresholds for products in surplus, and other measures to curb structural surpluses.

June 1984: At the Fontainebleau meeting of the European Council an agreement is reached on the amount of compensation to be granted to the United Kingdom to reduce its budget contribution.

September 15, 1984: Revision of ECU basket to include Greek drachma and to adjust weights of the other currencies.

June 1985: Agreement is reached on modifications of the EMS agreement enhancing the role of the ECU.

June 1985: The EC Commission submits White Paper on Completing the Internal Market, identifying almost 300 decisions needed to eliminate the physical, technical, and fiscal barriers preventing the formation of a complete common market and restricting EC competitiveness with the United States and Japan. Sets a timetable for decisions through the end of 1992.

January 1986: Accession of Spain and Portugal.

February 1986: Signing of the Single European Act, amending the Treaties establishing the European Communities. Act becomes effective in July 1987. Main objective is to complete the internal market. Also creates a streamlined decision-making process for the EC. The Act allows passage of Council decisions by qualified majority in most areas rather than unanimity and increases the role of the European Parliament.

April 1987: Turkey applies for EC membership.

September 1987: Basle/Nyborg Agreement. Central bank governors agree on measures liberalizing the financing of intramarginal interventions and on more flexible use of interest rates and fluctuation margins in case of exchange market pressure.

January/February 1988: Ministers Balladur (France), Amato (Italy), and Genscher (Germany) call for a strengthening of the EMS and the establishment of a European central bank.

January 1988: Commission proposes Second Banking Directive, which would allow banks to operate in any member state on a single license. Also increases the range of activities banks would be permitted to engage in (including activities in securities).

February 1988: At an emergency summit in Brussels, European Council reaches agreement on budget reforms. The final package adopted includes measures to cap the annual Community budget, restrain the annual rate of agricultural spending growth, scale back agricultural surpluses via overproduction penalties and set-asides, restructure the basis of budget contributions, and bolster the economies of the poorest regions through increased structural assistance.

June 13, 1988: Council of Ministers adopts a directive stipulating the complete liberalization of capital movements within the Community by July 1990. Extended transition periods granted to Portugal, Spain, Greece, and Ireland. Final approval on June 24, 1988.

June 27–28, 1988: At Hanover meeting, European Council establishes a committee of central bank governors and other experts to study/propose concrete stages toward economic and monetary union (EMU) for the EC. The committee, chaired by EC Commission President Jacques Delors, is scheduled to report to EC leaders at the June 1989 Madrid summit.

December 2–3, 1988: At the Rhodes meeting, European Council highlights remaining obstacles to completion of the internal market in the areas of indirect tax harmonization and social policy.

April 13, 1989: The EC Commission presents a revised version of the proposed Second Banking Directive. In the amended directive, which incorporates a more liberal formulation of reciprocity, banks from third countries providing "genuine national treatment" would not be prevented from entering the EC market. Genuine national treatment is defined as including "effective market access" and "competitive opportunities" for EC banks comparable to those available to domestic banks.

April 17, 1989: The Delors Committee submits final Report on Economic and Monetary Union in the European Community.

May 1989: By early May, the EC Commission submits to the Council of Ministers 232 of the 279 pieces of legislation identified in the 1985 White Paper, with final Council agreement reached on just over half of the total.

June 15 and 18, 1989: Direct elections are held for the 518 seats of the European Parliament. Elections hold added significance owing to the new powers granted to the Parliament over the internal market program in the Single European Act.

June 19, 1989: The EC Council of Ministers reaches agreement in principle on the Second Banking Directive to become effective at the beginning of 1993.

June 19, 1989: Spain joins exchange rate mechanism of the EMS, with a 6 percent fluctuation band as employed by the Italian lira.

June 26–27, 1989: At meeting in Madrid the European Council adopts the first stage of the Delors Report starting July 1, 1990 and requests that the competent bodies adopt the necessary provisions to initiate the first stage and organize an intergovernmental conference to initiate preparatory work required to "lay down the subsequent stages."

July 1989: Austria applies for EC membership.

September 21, 1989: Revision of the ECU basket to include the Portuguese escudo and the Spanish peseta and to adjust weights of the other currencies.

November 2, 1989: The British Chancellor of the Exchequer, John Major, rejects the idea of a single European currency and advocates a system of national currencies to compete within the framework of the EMS.

December 8–9, 1989: At a meeting in Strasbourg the European Council formally agrees on convening an Intergovernmental Conference (IGC) on EMU in December 1990 to prepare the institutional changes for stages two and three of the proposals of the Delors Committee.

December 15, 1989: The Second Banking Directive is approved unanimously by the EC Council of Ministers. Member countries are to adapt their laws and regulations to reach compliance with the directive by January 1, 1993.

January 1, 1990: France abolishes remaining restrictions on capital movements ahead of July 1 deadline.

January 8, 1990: Italy adopts narrow margins within the ERM, together with a modest devaluation of the central rate of the lira.

March 2, 1990: Belgium and Luxembourg abolish dual exchange markets for the Belgian-Luxembourg francs.

March 12, 1990: In preparation for EMU, EC finance ministers amend the decisions of 1974 and 1964, respectively, concerning economic convergence and cooperation between central banks.

March 20, 1990: The Commission sets out detailed ideas on EMU ("Economic Monetary Union: The Economic Rationale and Design of the System").

March 31/April 1, 1990: Meeting of EC finance ministers and central bank governors reveals considerable agreement on a future economic and monetary union and on the ultimate objective of economic and monetary union.

April 28, 1990: The European Council at a special meeting in Dublin states that it is "satisfied with progress achieved so far towards establishing the single market without frontiers" and asks the intergovernmental conference on EMU to "conclude its work rapidly with the objective of ratification [of the Treaty amendment] by member states before the end of 1992," to coincide with the envisaged completion of the internal market. The Council confirms "its commitment to Political Union" and sets in motion an examination of treaty changes, with the aim of strengthening the democratic legitimacy of the union, by a second intergovernmental conference to work in parallel with the IGC on EMU.

May 14, 1990: Italy abolishes remaining restrictions on capital movements ahead of July 1 deadline.

June 1990: The Belgian Government decides to tie the value of the Belgian franc to the deutsche mark.

June 25–26, 1990: At a meeting in Dublin, the European Council calls for the convening of two intergovernmental conferences on EMU and on political union in mid-December. The Council also welcomes progress toward completion of the internal market and calls for further progress in the areas of public procurement, investment services and insurance, and intellectual property.

July 1, 1990: EC member states have to comply with the directive stipulating the complete liberalization of capital movements. Beginning of the first stage of the process (as suggested in the Delors Report) leading to EMU.

July 1990: Cyprus and Malta apply for EC membership.

October 8, 1990: Sterling enters the ERM of the EMS. The U.K. Government adopts a margin of fluctuation of 6 percent and pledges to adopt the narrow margin of 2¼ percent after an adjustment period.

October 22, 1990: Norway links its currency, the krone, to the ECU and will allow the currency to fluctuate within a narrow band of 2¼ percent of its central rate with the ECU.

October 1990: The European Commission publishes a report ("One Market, One Money") evaluating the economic costs and benefits of EMU.

October 27–28, 1990: At a European Council meeting in Rome, EC countries, except the United Kingdom, agree to start second stage toward EMU on January 1, 1994, and to establish a new monetary institution at the beginning of this stage.

December 14, 1990: Intergovernmental conferences on EMU and political union scheduled to begin.

Bibliography

Alesina, Alberto, "Politics and business cycles in industrial democracies," *Economic Policy* (April 1989).

Amato, Giuliano, "Un motore per lo Sme," *Il Sole 24 Ore* (Milan), February 25, 1988.

Artis, Michael J., and Mark P. Taylor, "The Achievements of the European Monetary System," *Economic and Social Review*, Vol. 20, No. 2 (January 1989).

Balladur, Edouard, "Mémorandum sur la construction monétaire européenne," *ECU*, No. 3 (Brussels, March 1988).

Bank of England, "Memorandum on the Delors Report," *BIS Review*, June 26, 1989, p. 4 (also *Auszüge aus Presseartikeln*, Deutsche Bundesbank, July 6, 1989).

Basevi, Giorgio, "Monetary Cooperation and Liberalization of Capital Movements in the European Monetary System," *European Economic Review*, Vol. 32 (March 1988).

———, Michele Fratianni, Herbert Giersch, Pieter Korteweg, David O'Mahony, Michael Parkin, Theo Peeters, Pascal Salin, and Niels Thygesen, "The All Saints' day manifesto for European monetary union," *The Economist*, November 1, 1975.

Blunden, George, The Julian Hodge Bank Annual Lecture, University of Wales, Cardiff, February 14, 1990, *BIS Review*, No. 39, February 23, 1990.

Bofinger, Peter, "Problems of European Policy Coordination in the Transitional Phase," in *European Monetary Integration: From German Dominance to an EC Central Bank?* ed. by Paul J.J. Welfens (Heidelberg: Springer, 1990).

Bredenkamp, Hugh, and Michael Deppler, "Fiscal Constraints of a Fixed Exchange Rate Regime," in *Choosing an Exchange Rate Regime: The Challenge for Smaller Industrial Countries*, ed. by Victor Argy and Paul De Grauwe (Washington: International Monetary Fund, 1990).

Brittan, Samuel, "Why evolution is a better route to Emu," *Financial Times*, November 13, 1989.

———, "How to save Ecu plan," *Financial Times*, July 5, 1990.

Caballero, Ricardo J., and Vittorio Corbo, "The Effect of Real Exchange Rate Uncertainty on Exports: Empirical Evidence," *World Bank Economic Review*, Vol. 3 (May 1989).

Carli, Guido, "Co-ordination, not competition," *Financial Times*, January 17, 1990.

Chalikias, Dimitrios, Interview with *Handelsblatt Wirtschafts- und Finanzzeitung*, July 13/14, 1990.

Chowdhury, Abdur R., and Fabio Sdogati, "Has the European Monetary System Been Instrumental for the Convergence of Inflation Rates in Europe?" (unpublished; Marquette University, Milwaukee, 1990).

Ciampi, Carlo A., "The Revival of the Italian Economy: Strengths and Weaknesses," Address to the Round Table organized by Business International, Rome, January 26, 1988, *Economic Bulletin*, Banca d'Italia, No. 6 (February 1988).

——— (1989a), Speech in Bad Neuenahr, October 18, 1989, *BIS Review*, No. 218, November 7, 1989.

——— (1989b), Lecture at the University of Macerata on November 29, 1989, *BIS Review*, No. 244, December 13, 1989.

Cohen, Daniel, Jacques Melitz, and Gilles Oudiz, "Le système monétaire européen et l'asymétrie franc-mark," *Revue Economique*, Vol. 39 (May 1988).

Collins, Susan M., "Inflation and the European Monetary System," in *The European Monetary System*, ed. by Francesco Giavazzi, Stefano Micossi, and Marcus Miller (Cambridge: Cambridge University Press, 1988).

Commission of the European Communities, *Optica Report '75—Towards Economic Equilibrium and Monetary Unification in Europe* (Brussels, January 16, 1976).

———, *Optica Report 1976—Inflation and Exchange Rates: Evidence and Policy Guidelines for the European Community* (Brussels, February 10, 1977).

———, "The European Monetary System—Commentary and Documents," *European Economy*, No. 3 (July 1979).

———, "Documents relating to the European Monetary System," *European Economy*, No. 12 (July 1982).

———, "Creation of a European Financial Area," *European Economy*, No. 36 (May 1988).

——— (1989a), "The EMS—Ten Years of Progress in European Monetary Cooperation" (Brussels, 1989).

——— (1989b), Annual Economic Report, 1989–90, *European Economy*, No. 42 (November 1989).

——— (1990a), "Economic and Monetary Union: The Economic Rationale and Design of the System," Press Release, Brussels, March 20, 1990.

——— (1990b), "Economic and Monetary Union: The Economic Rationale and Design of the System," Europe Documents, March 23, 1990, *BIS Review*, March 28 and March 30, 1990.

_____ (1990c), "One Market, One Money," *European Economy*, No. 44 (October 1990).

Committee for the Monetary Union of Europe, A Programme for Action (June 1988).

Committee for the Study of Economic and Monetary Union (Delors Committee), *Report on Economic and Monetary Union in the European Community* (Luxembourg, April 1989).

Costa, Antonio, Presentation at the CBI Conference on European Monetary Union, London, October 10, 1989, *BIS Review*, No. 230 (November 23, 1989).

Currie, David, "Competition in policies, not currencies," *Financial Times*, November 15, 1989.

de Cecco, Marcello, and Alberto Giovannini, eds., *A European Central Bank? Perspectives on monetary unification after ten years of the EMS* (Cambridge: Cambridge University Press, 1989).

De Grauwe, Paul (1989a), "Is the European Monetary System a DM-Zone?" Discussion Paper Series No. 297 (Brussels: Centre for European Policy Studies, March 1989).

_____ (1989b), "Liberalization of Capital Movements and the EMS," paper presented at a conference "The European Monetary System, Ten Years Later," University of Bergamo, May 1989.

_____, and Theo Peeters, eds., *The ECU and European Monetary Integration* (Basingstoke, England: Macmillan, 1989).

de Larosière, Jacques (1990a), "European Economic and Monetary Union: What Is at Stake," speech to the Siparex Club, Lyon, February 26, 1990, *Auszüge aus Presseartikeln*, Deutsche Bundesbank, March 19, 1990.

_____ (1990b), "Les finalités et modalités de la création d'un système européen de banques centrales," intervention au 8e congrès du Comité des syndicats des banques centrales européennes à Marne-la-Vallée, March 27, 1990, *BIS Review*, No. 66, April 3, 1990.

Deutsche Bundesbank, "Exchange Rate Movements Within the European Monetary System—Experience After Ten Years," *Monthly Report*, November 1989.

_____, "Statement by the Deutsche Bundesbank on the Establishment of an Economic and Monetary Union in Europe," *Monthly Report,* October 1990.

_____, *Annual Reports*, various issues.

Deville, Volker, *The European Monetary System and the European Currency Unit: Bibliography,* 2nd rev. ed., European University Institute, Working Paper No. 86/206 (Florence, 1986).

Dini, Lamberto, Statement for the Committee on Economic and Monetary Affairs and Industrial Policy of the European Parliament, Brussels, July 13, 1988, *BIS Review*, July 14, 1988.

Doyle, Maurice, "Economic and Monetary Union," speech at the Association of Chartered Accountants, Cork, March 9, 1990, *Auszüge aus Presseartikeln*, Deutsche Bundesbank, March 16, 1990.

Driffill, John, "The Stability and Sustainability of the European Monetary System with Perfect Capital Markets," in *The European Monetary System*, ed. by Francesco Giavazzi, Stefano Micossi, and Marcus Miller (Cambridge: Cambridge University Press, 1988).

Duisenberg, W.F., "Merits of Monetary Stability," speech at the American Chamber of Commerce, The Hague, June 1, 1988, De Nederlandsche Bank, *Quarterly Bulletin*, No. 1 (June 1988).

_____ (1989a), "The ECU as a Parallel Currency," Delors Report, pp. 185–89.

_____ (1989b), Interview, *Finanz und Wirtschaft*, October 11, 1989 (English translation in *BIS Review*, No. 213, October 31, 1989).

The Economist, "Economic and monetary union: Hold on a minute," November 4, 1989, pp. 58–59.

Edison, Hali J., and Eric Fisher, "A Long-Run View of the European Monetary System," International Finance Discussion Papers, No. 339 (Board of Governors of the Federal Reserve System, January 1989).

Eltis, Walter, "The Obstacles to European Monetary Union," *International Currency Review*, Vol. 20 (August-September 1989).

European Communities, *Official Journal of the European Communities* (Luxembourg), various issues.

European Parliament, Committee on Economic and Monetary Affairs and Industrial Policy, *Report on the Development of European Monetary Integration*, January 1989.

Feldstein, Martin, "Economics in Government: Thinking About International Economic Coordination," *Auszüge aus Presseartikeln*, Deutsche Bundesbank, July 15, 1988.

Financial Times, "UK Rejection of Delors Plan Threatens EC Unity," April 18, 1989.

Folkerts-Landau, David, and Donald J. Mathieson, *The European Monetary System in the Context of the Integration of European Financial Markets*, Occasional Paper No. 66 (Washington: International Monetary Fund, 1989).

Fratianni, Michele, and Jürgen von Hagen, "German Dominance in the EMS: The Empirical Evidence," *Open Economies Review* (January 1990).

Genscher, Hans-Dietrich, "Memorandum für die Schaffung eines europäischen Währungsraumes und einer Europäischen Zentralbank" *Auszüge aus Presseartikeln*, Deutsche Bundesbank, March 1, 1988.

Giavazzi, Francesco, "European Monetary System: Lessons from Europe and Perspectives in Europe," *Economic and Social Review*, Vol. 20 (January 1989).

_____, and Alberto Giovannini, "The Role of the Exchange-Rate Regime in a Disinflation: Empirical Evidence on the European Monetary System," in *The European Monetary System*, ed. by Francesco Giavazzi, Stefano Micossi, and Marcus Miller (Cambridge: Cambridge University Press, 1988).

Giavazzi, Francesco, and Marco Pagano, "The Advantage of Tying One's Hands: EMS Discipline and Central Bank Credibility," *European Economic Review*, Vol. 32 (June 1988).

Giavazzi, Francesco, Stefano Micossi, and Marcus Miller, eds., *The European Monetary System* (Cambridge: Cambridge University Press, 1988).

Gleske, Leonhard, "Die Liberalisierung des Kapitalverkehrs in der EG," *Auszüge aus Presseartikeln,* Deutsche Bundesbank, July 9, 1986.

———, "Die Fortentwicklung des Europäischen Währungssystems," Ausführungen vor dem Ausschuss für Wirtschaft, Währung und Industriepolitik des Europäischen Parlaments (Brussels, February 22, 1988), *Auszüge aus Presseartikeln,* No. 15, Deutsche Bundesbank, March 1, 1988.

Gressani, Daniela, Luigi Guiso, and Ignazio Visco, "Disinflation in Italy: An Analysis with the Econometric Model of the Bank of Italy," *Journal of Policy Modeling,* Vol. 10, No. 2 (1988).

Gros, Daniel, and Niels Thygesen, *The EMS: Achievements, Current Issues and Directions for the Future,* CEPS Paper No. 35 (Brussels: Centre for European Policy Studies, 1988).

Guitián, Manuel, "The European Monetary System: A Balance Between Rules and Discretion," Part I in *Policy Coordination in the European Monetary System,* Occasional Paper No. 61 (Washington: International Monetary Fund, 1988).

Harbrecht, Wolfgang, and Jürgen Schmid, "Die Beziehungen zwischen Wechselkursstabilisierung und wirtschaftlicher Konvergenz," Veröffentlichungen des HWWA-Institut für Wirtschaftsforschung (Hamburg: Verlag Weltarchiv Gmbh, 1988).

Hasse, Rolf, "Die ECU—ein Währungsmedium mit Integrationswirkungen?" *Zeitschrift für Wirtschaftspolitik,* Heft 2–3 (Cologne, 1988).

International Monetary Fund, *Exchange Rate Volatility and World Trade: A Study by the Research Department of the International Monetary Fund,* Occasional Paper No. 28 (Washington: International Monetary Fund, 1984).

———, *The Role of the SDR in the International Monetary System,* Part Two: A Comparative Analysis of the Functions of the ECU and the SDR, Occasional Paper No. 51 (Washington: International Monetary Fund, 1987).

Istituto Bancario San Paolo di Torino, *ECU Newsletter,* various issues.

Johansson, Sven-Olof, "The Issue of an Economic and Monetary Union within the EC," Sveriges Riksbank, *Quarterly Review,* Vol. 4, No. 2 (1988).

Jones, Susan, "Fiscal Reforms and EMS Participation Contribute to Ireland's Stability and Growth," *IMF Survey,* International Monetary Fund (Washington), January 22, 1990.

Kloten, Norbert, "Wege zu einem Europäischen Zentralbanksystem," *Europa-Archiv: Zeitschrift für Internationale Politik,* Folge 11 (1988) (English translation in *BIS Review,* July 19, 1988).

———, and Peter Bofinger, "Währungsintegration über eine europäische Parallelwährung," *Europa-Banking,* ed. by D. Duwendag (Baden-Baden, 1988).

———, "Perspektiven der europäischen Währungsintegration," *Jahrbücher für Nationalökonomie und Statistik,* Band 206, Heft 4–5 (October 1989).

Kremers, Jeroen J.M., "Gaining Policy Credibility for a Disinflation: Ireland's Experience in the EMS," International Monetary Fund, *Staff Papers,* Vol. 37, No. 1 (March 1990).

———, and Timothy D. Lane, "Economic and Monetary Integration and the Aggregate Demand for Money in the EMS," Working Paper No. 90/23 (Washington: International Monetary Fund, March 1990).

Leigh-Pemberton, Robin, "The Future of Monetary Arrangements in Europe," Bank of England, *Quarterly Bulletin,* Vol. 29, No. 3 (August 1989).

Levich, Richard M., ed., *ECU—European Currency Unit* (London: Euromoney Publications, 1987).

Lindenius, Christina, Peter Norman, and Åke Törnqvist, "European Monetary Cooperation—Function and Development," Sveriges Riksbank, *Quarterly Review,* Vol. 4, No. 2 (1988).

Lipschitz, Leslie, and Donogh McDonald, "Real Exchange Rates and Competitiveness: A Clarification of Concepts and Some Measurements for Europe," IMF Working Paper (Washington: International Monetary Fund, forthcoming 1990).

Major, John, "Economic and Monetary Union: Beyond Stage One," speech to German Industry Forum, London, June 20, 1990.

Mayer, Joerg, "Capital Controls in the EMS—A Survey," CEPS Working Document No. 43 (Brussels: Centre for European Policy Studies, August 1989).

McDonald, Frank, and others, "The European Monetary System: Towards 1992 and Beyond," *Journal of Common Market Studies,* Vol. 27, No. 3 (March 1988).

Melitz, J., "Monetary Discipline and Cooperation in the European Monetary System: A Synthesis," in *The European Monetary System,* ed. by Francesco Giavazzi, Stefano Micossi, and Marcus Miller (Cambridge: Cambridge University Press, 1988).

Moss, Frank, "EC central banks and private ECU interventions," ECU Banking Association, *EBA Newsletter* (January 1988).

Padoa-Schioppa, Tommaso, "The European Monetary System: A Long-Term View," in *The European Monetary System,* ed. by Francesco Giavazzi, Stefano Micossi, and Marcus Miller (Cambridge: Cambridge University Press, 1988).

Pöhl, Karl Otto (1990a), "Grundzüge einer europäischen Geldordnung," speech, January 16, 1990, Paris, *Auszüge aus Presseartikeln,* Deutsche Bundesbank, January 16, 1990 (English version in *BIS Review,* No. 12, January 17, 1990).

——— (1990b), Interview with *The Times,* London, June 26, 1990.

Portes, Richard, "Macroeconomic Policy Coordination and the European Monetary System," paper presented at a conference, "The European Monetary System, Ten Years Later," University of Bergamo, May 1989.

Rey, Jean-Jacques, "Discussion of Collins," in *The European Monetary System,* ed. by Franceso Giavazzi,

Stefano Micossi, and Marcus Miller (Cambridge: Cambridge University Press, 1988).

Rieke, Wolfgang, "The European Monetary System," paper presented at a seminar, "New Developments in Banking and Finance in East and West," organized by the Austrian National Bank and the Vienna Institute for Comparative Economic Studies, Gloggnitz (Austria), October 10–13, 1989.

Rogoff, Kenneth, "Can Exchange Rate Predictability Be Achieved Without Monetary Convergence? Evidence from the EMS," *European Economic Review*, Vol. 28 (June/July 1985).

Russo, Massimo, "Cooperation and Coordination in the EMS—The System at a Crossroad," in *Internationales Währungssystem und weltwirtschaftliche Entwicklung (The International Monetary System and Economic Development)*, Proceedings from Malente Symposion VII (Baden-Baden: Nomos Verlagsgesellschaft, 1988).

——, and Giuseppe Tullio, "Monetary Coordination Within the European Monetary System: Is There a Rule?" Part II in *Policy Coordination in the European Monetary System*, Occasional Paper No. 61 (Washington: International Monetary Fund, 1988).

Scharrer, Hans Eckart, "Das EWS—Ein Beispiel erfolgreicher Wirtschaftskooperation?" in *Internationales Währungssystem und weltwirtschaftliche Entwicklung (The International Monetary System and Economic Development)*, Proceedings from Malente Symposion VII (Baden-Baden: Nomos Verlagsgesellschaft, 1988).

Schinasi, Garry J., "European Integration, Exchange Rates and Monetary Reform," *World Economy*, Vol. 12, No. 4 (December 1989).

Schröder, Wolfgang, "Will Continuing Liberalisation in the EC lead to Instability in the EMS?" *Intereconomics* (July/August 1989).

Steinherr, Alfred, "The EMS with the ECU at Centre Stage: A Proposal for Reform of the European Exchange Rate System," European University Institute, Working Paper No. 88/339 (Florence, 1988).

Stoltenberg, Gerhard, "The further development of monetary cooperation in Europe," Press Release, Federal Ministry of Finance (Bonn, March 15, 1988).

Szász, A., "European Monetary Integration Beyond 1992," speech at the European Finance Symposium, Antwerp, November 4, 1988, De Nederlandsche Bank, *Quarterly Bulletin*, 1988/3 (December 1988).

Thygesen, Niels, "Introduction," in *The European Monetary System*, ed. by Francesco Giavazzi, Stefano Micossi, and Marcus Miller (Cambridge: Cambridge University Press, 1988).

Ungerer, Horst, "The European Monetary System," *IMF Survey*, International Monetary Fund (Washington), March 19, 1979, Supplement.

——, "The European Monetary System and the International Monetary System," *Journal of Common Market Studies*, Vol. 27 (March 1989).

—— (1990a), "The EMS, 1979–1990: Policies—Evolution—Outlook," *Konjunkturpolitik,* Heft 6/1990.

—— (1990b), "Comments on Peter Bofinger," in *European Monetary Integration: From German Dominance to an EC Central Bank?* ed. by Paul J.J. Welfens (Heidelberg: Springer, 1990).

——, Owen Evans, and Peter Nyberg, *The European Monetary System: The Experience, 1979–82*, Occasional Paper No. 19 (Washington: International Monetary Fund, 1983).

Ungerer, Horst, Owen Evans, Thomas Mayer, and Philip Young, *The European Monetary System: Recent Developments*, Occasional Paper No. 48 (Washington: International Monetary Fund, 1986).

United Kingdom (1989a), House of Commons, *Hansard*, Vol. 155, No. 32, June 12 and 29, 1989 (London: Her Majesty's Stationery Office, 1989).

—— (1989b), H.M. Treasury, "An Evolutionary Approach to Economic and Monetary Union" (London, November 1989).

Vaubel, Roland, "Strategies for Currency Unification—The Economics of Currency Competition and the Case for a European Parallel Currency," Tübingen, 1978.

Welfens, Paul J.J., ed., *European Monetary Integration: From German Dominance to an EC Central Bank?* (Heidelberg: Springer, 1990).

Williamson, John, "The Exchange Rate System," Institute for International Economics, Policy Analyses, *International Economics*, No. 5 (Washington, 2nd ed., 1985).

Wissenschaftlicher Beirat beim Bundesministerium für Wirtschaft (1989a) (Board of Academic Advisers to the Federal Ministry of Economics), "Europäische Währungsordnung" ("A Monetary Order for the Single European Market") (Bonn), January 21, 1989.

—— (1989b), "Stellungnahme zum Delors-Bericht," *Bundesanzeiger* (Bonn), July 1, 1989.

Wyplosz, Charles (1988a), "The EMS—From Success to Transition," in *Internationales Währungssystem und weltwirtschaftliche Entwicklung (The International Monetary System and Economic Development)*, Proceedings from Malente Symposion VII (Baden-Baden: Nomos Verlagsgesellschaft, 1988).

—— (1988b), "Capital flow liberalization and the EMS: A French perspective," Commission of the European Communities, *European Economy*, No. 36, 1988.

——, "Asymmetry in the EMS: Intentional or Systemic?" *European Economic Review*, Vol. 33 (March 1989).